SUCCESS IN THE YEAR OF THE PIG

[2019 EDITION]

Linda Dearsley

DARK RIVER

TABLE OF CONTENTS

CHAPTER 1: SUCCESS IN THE YEAR OF THE PIG

Welcome to the Chinese New Year of the Pig which begins – if you're the organised type who likes to plan ahead, or began, in case you're the laid-back sort who doesn't believe in rushing these things – on the 5th of February 2019 and which runs right through until January 24th 2020.

Now it's true that, here in the West, the Year of the Pig may not sound an appealing prospect – but according to Chinese lore, our unthinking prejudices are completely wrong. In fact, Pig years are particularly welcome in the East as they're believed to usher in a time of plenty. So what will 2019 bring to you? Will the cheerful Pig present you with a trough full of golden goodies? Or could you end up wallowing in a grubby sty?

2019 - A Joyous Feast of Fun?

Despite the sometimes unflattering connotations of the term 'pig' in the West ('It's been a pig of a day', anyone? 'I've just scrapped that pig of a car', and so on) the Chinese regard 'Pig' years as particularly auspicious.

Of course, there's always something exciting about the start of a brand new year – any new year. There's that optimistic feeling in the air that a fresh new page has been turned, and that we can put the past behind us and begin again, forging a brighter new future.

That hopeful mood strikes most of us every new year. But at the dawn of the Year of the Pig, there's even more reason than usual to feel good about the coming 12 months.

The Year of the Pig is special partly because it's regarded as a year of abundance and partly because of its unique place in the Chinese celestial calendar.

Every Year is Different – from Day One

It sometimes seems as if our familiar Western Astrology pays little attention to the turn of a new year. Focusing as it does on the movement of the planets from week to week, month to month, and the changing influences they beam to us on Earth as they pass, it's easy to regard the actual year as little more than a man-made date – a series of numbers of no great significance to these majestic power-players of the universe.

Yet to Chinese astrologers it's just the opposite. The year itself is of *enormous importance*. Each year arrives with a distinct 'personality' already fully formed from day one – the personality of one of the 12 celestial animals that make up the Chinese calendar. Each of these animals has its own individual character, completely different from that of the animal that went before, and it's this special character that sets the tone, the mood for the entire year ahead. So every New Year's Day, a totally different energy is unleashed on the world, and this new energy will influence events as they unfold for the whole of the next twelve months.

Circumstances that might have led to dangerous disputes in a fiery Tiger year could pass by with scarcely a ripple when peaceful Rabbit is running the show. A little bit of devious disregard for the rules in a good cause might be overlooked in a Rat year, but when 'do-the-right-thing' Dog is in charge, retribution will be swift and unpleasant.

The twelve celestial animals of the East have been rotating in the same order in an endless cycle through the centuries for possibly 3,000 years, each getting their turn to rule the world in their own unique way, once every twelve years.

The New Year's Party that Lasts All Year

The great thing about Pig years is that the Pig is the twelfth sign of the zodiac. The Pig always arrives at the very end of the long, twelve-year cycle which began over a decade before, with the energetic sign of the Rat.

By the time the Year of the Pig comes round we've had enough. We've put in years and years of hard work, years of effort and struggle, now we can sense it's time to ease up, sit back, and hopefully enjoy the fruits of our labours. There's an end of term feeling in the air. That last day of school euphoria, or maybe a dash of New Year's Eve craziness.

Okay, so in 2020 we know the cycle begins all over again when Rat rushes back to kick-start a new era, but we don't want to think about that now. We don't need to think about that for another twelve whole months! For now, we just want to kick off our shoes and party. At last, we can enjoy a well-deserved break and have some fun.

Different Pigs For Different Years

Since pigs usually have very large litters, they're regarded as a symbol of abundance, so all Pig years are expected to bring months of plenty. Yet just as a Lamborghini car is completely different from a Mini in appearance and style, while still sharing the same basic car characteristics, so not all Pig years are exactly the same in character.

2019 is the year of the Earth Pig, or Brown Pig – a rare beast. Brown Pig has not put in an appearance since 1959. It's been 60 long years since Brown Pig last trotted over the horizon so unless you're well into your sixth decade, you're unlikely to remember much about it.

So what was going on in 1959 that might give us a clue as to what to expect from its 2019 cousin?

Meet The Last Brown Pig

For a start, the principal world leaders remained unchanged from the previous year. Dwight Eisenhower was still president of the USA, Harold Macmillan or 'SuperMac' as he became known, was still Prime Minister of Britain (and even went on to win another term in the general election of October 1959), Nikita Khrushchev was still Premier of the Soviet Union, and young Queen Elizabeth was settling into her role as Monarch of Great Britain and the Commonwealth.

True, Fidel Castro was officially sworn in as President of Cuba during the year of the Pig but he'd actually seized power over a month before, towards the end of the previous Chinese Year – the Year of the Dog – so technically he was already running the country by the time the Year of the Pig arrived.

Intriguingly, three of the top people in the news that year – Eisenhower, Castro and Queen Elizabeth – were born under the sign of the Tiger while the other two – Macmillan and Khrushchev – were both Chinese zodiac Horses. So if you're a Chinese Tiger or Horse, it could be a good omen.

The zodiac Pig is associated with a love of ease, creature comforts, and frivolity, while the Earth element represents stability and family values. So perhaps it's not surprising the world leaders of '59 remained unchanged from the previous year, lending an air of stability to proceedings, and that 1959 was the year a number of small-scale but delightfully family-friendly innovations were launched.

The Brown Pig welcomed in 'Pantyhose' or 'tights' which freed women from the discomfort of the draughty suspender belt and stockings, Barbie (the Barbie Doll) made her first appearance, thrilling small girls everywhere, and the cute yet practical Mini rolled onto the road for the first time, priced at an astonishing £500 – making driving affordable for all. To help motorists make the most of such freedom, a couple of months later, the first section of the M1 motorway was opened near Toddington in Bedfordshire. And just in case all this speed tempted drivers to get reckless, Volvo produced the first ever car with three-point seat belts for safety.

Rawhide and Bonanza – both homely, cowboy-themed Westerns – were delighting audiences on TV. Ben-Hur and Some Like it Hot with Marilyn Monroe were the big hits in the cinema, Cliff Richard's Living Doll was the year's top-selling single in the UK, and on Broadway, a brand new show about a family of singers opened. It was called The Sound of Music.

Meanwhile, at Disneyland, the original family playground, Walt Disney unveiled the resort's futuristic Monorail – an event so momentous it seemed, he managed to secure the Vice President of the USA no less, (one Richard Nixon) to take the first ride, along with Nixon's wife and daughters.

And just to underline the family theme, that August, Queen Elizabeth announced she was pregnant with her third child. (Prince Andrew was born the following February).

Even the most talked-about scandals of the year, in the USA at least, concerned such domestic outrages as the fixing of popular TV quiz shows and the paying of radio stations to plug particular records, 'Payola' as the practice became known.

While the year had its share of floods, storms, and accidents, looking back on that time now, 1959 seems to exude a sense of cosiness and simple pleasures and perhaps, the end of an era. Just what you'd expect from the Year of the Pig.

The 2019 Brown Pig

So will our new Brown Pig bring a lucky year? How will the piggy influences affect the world in 2019? If it was possible for a zodiac year to arrive with a mission statement, the Year of the Pig's would probably be: 'Eat, Drink and be Merry,' plus 'Go on, spoil yourself. You're worth it.'

All around, there's a lightening of mood. After the serious, conscientious Year of the Dog in 2018, there's a more relaxed feel in the air. People seem to recover their sense of humour; they make more time to be friendly.

Pigs are sensitive creatures; they dislike dramatic events, big changes and general unpleasantness so, politically perhaps, we can expect a calmer year with diplomacy taking precedence over discord. There's an emphasis on the pleasures of life: entertainment, luxury items of all varieties, feel-good treats, and tasty food will be in the spotlight.

But due to Brown Pig's earth influence, these will be expressed in a homely, security-conscious way.

We'll be drawn to frequent holidays and short breaks but not necessarily far afield or exotic. The Pig is not particularly adventurous so spa resorts, cruises, and safe, all-in package trips could be especially enticing this year. Beauty therapies, hairdressing, undemanding health regimes, fashion and nutrition will be prominent – as will dancing and comedy. Although they're not martyrs to fitness, Pigs do love to dance, and they love to laugh. Comedians should do very well in 2019.

Food, of course, will be particularly important. Restaurants, cookery shows, foodie shops and products can expect to find business booming, but there's also likely to be an even greater concern for the earth itself and how our food is produced. Farming and farming methods will assume even greater importance and any hint of contamination or adulteration of food will result in scandal.

Last year's desire for pure, natural products is likely to intensify, as is concern about pollution and the environment.

Although this year's Pig is an Earth Pig, all the zodiac Pigs are believed to belong to the Water element as well, so determination to clean up our seas and waterways is another theme that's likely to grow stronger. Stand by for scientific developments aimed at solving the problem of plastic dumped in the oceans, and saving the planet's coral reefs. On the business front, there could be the announcement of several even larger, more luxurious cruise ships.

TV, the cinema, theme parks, and the seaside will prove hugely attractive, and since Pigs love to have hordes of happy little piglets around them, there could be a boom in children's entertainment and a new toy craze. Even adults without children could find the urge to indulge their inner child irresistible this year.

Fittingly, the Year of the Pig will see the birth of the latest member of the Royal Family when the Duchess of Sussex's baby arrives in the Spring.

Shopaholics Watch Out

Yet though 2019 looks very promising in many ways, no year can ever be perfect and Pig years have their flaws. Most of all, the impulse to spend, spend, spend can be dangerous to personal bank balances and disastrous to national economies. 2019 could throw up a number of financial crises with international repercussions. Governments will be tempted to overspend recklessly with little thought given to how the debt can be repaid.

Pigs are notorious for failing to plan sufficiently far ahead, and they tend to be careless with details. Their 'live for the day' philosophy may be fun, but it can lead to big trouble a few months down the line.

We could see big companies suddenly crashing, apparently without warning, another banking crisis, and governments piling up unaffordable debt with unpopular consequences. What's more, the Pig's lack of attention to boring details could cause large-scale and expensive projects to collapse unexpectedly, due to complications that should have been foreseen at the planning stage but which were somehow overlooked.

Ironically the Pig's carefree, happy-go-lucky desire to avoid unpleasant situations can actually create just the sort of convoluted problems they were hoping to avoid. This year, we could see a number of big legal scandals as a result.

On a personal level, it could be very difficult to keep a tight grip on our credit cards and the temptation to overindulge could see our waistlines bulging. What's more, we're even less inclined than usual to commit to regular vigorous exercise.

Last year was also an Earth year, but the quality of Earth in 2019 is much milder and gentler than it was in 2018. This is the kind of Earth associated with gently rolling fields and fertile farmland rather than towering mountains, but since the Pig is also linked with Water, there could be problems with flooding, particularly in low-lying areas, right from the start of the year.

How the Years Got their Names

According to Chinese folklore, there are many explanations as to why the calendar is divided up the way it is. Perhaps the most popular is the story about the supreme Jade Emperor who lives in heaven. He decided to name each year in honour of a different animal and decreed that a race would be run to decide which animals would be chosen, and the order in which they would appear.

Twelve animals arrived to take part. Actually, in one legend there were 13, and included the cat, at the time a great friend of the rat. But the cat was a sleepy creature and asked the rat to wake him in time for the race and in the excitement (or was it by design?) the rat forgot and dashed off leaving the cat fast asleep. The cat missed the race and missed out on getting a year dedicated to his name. Which is why cats have hated rats ever since.

Anyway, as they approached the finish line, the 12 competitors found a wide river blocking their route. The powerful Ox, a strong swimmer, plunged straight in, but the tiny Rat begged to be carried across on his back. Kindly Ox agreed, but when they reached the opposite bank, the wily Rat scampered down Ox's body, jumped off his head and shot across the finish line in first place. Which is why the Rat is the first animal of the Chinese zodiac, followed by the Ox.

The muscular Tiger, weighed down by his magnificent coat, arrived in third place, followed by the non-swimming Rabbit who'd found some rocks downstream and hopped neatly from one to another to reach dry land.

The Emperor was surprised to see the Dragon with his great wings, fly in in fifth place instead of the expected first. The Dragon explained that while high up in the sky he saw a village in flames and the people running out of their houses in great distress, so he'd made a detour and employed his rain-making skills (Chinese Dragons can create water as well as fire) to put out the blaze before returning to the race.

In sixth place came the Snake. Clever as the Rat, the Snake had wrapped himself around one of the Horse's hooves and hung on while the Horse swam the river. When the Horse climbed ashore, the Snake slithered off, so startling the Horse that it reared up in alarm, allowing the Snake to slide over the finish line ahead of him.

The Goat, Monkey, and Rooster arrived next at the river. They spotted some driftwood and rope washed up on the shore, so Monkey deftly lashed them together to make a raft and the three of them hopped aboard and floated across. The Goat jumped off first, swiftly followed by Monkey and Rooster. They found they'd beaten the Dog which was unexpected as the Dog was a good swimmer.

It turned out the Dog so enjoyed the water, he'd hung around playing in the shallows emerging only in time to come eleventh. Last of all came the Pig, not the best of swimmers and further slowed by his decision to pause for a good meal before exerting himself in the current.

And so the wheel of the zodiac was set for evermore, with the Year of the Rat beginning the cycle, followed by the Ox, Tiger, Rabbit, Dragon, Snake, Horse, Goat, Monkey, Rooster, Dog and Pig.

Chinese Horoscope Signs

It's thought that originally, an understanding of astrology was considered useful only to rulers and their advisors as a guide to planning the affairs of the nation for the year ahead. But over the centuries people realised astrology could be used on a personal level too. They believed that the animal ruling the year in which you were born, left an indelible imprint on your personality and destiny. And therefore, whether your animal birth sign was a friend or foe of the animal ruling the year ahead – there could be big differences to your prospects that year.

How to Succeed in 2019

So, since 2019 is the Year of the Pig, how will you fare? Does the Pig present your astrological animal with opportunities or challenges? As the fable about how the years got their names shows, every one of the astrological animals is resourceful in its own special way. Faced with the daunting prospect of crossing the river, each successfully made it to the other side, even the creatures that could barely swim.

So whether your year animal gets on easily with the Brown Pig, or whether they have to work at their relationship, you can make 2019 a wonderful year to remember.

Chinese Astrology has been likened to a weather forecast. Once you know whether you need your umbrella or your suntan lotion, you can set out with confidence and enjoy the trip.

Find Your Chinese Astrology Sign

To find your Chinese sign just look up your birth year in the table below.

Important note: if you were born in January or February, check the dates of the New Year very carefully. The Chinese New Year follows the lunar calendar and the beginning and end dates are not fixed, but vary each year. If you were born before mid-February, your animal sign might actually be the sign of the previous year. For example, 1980 was the year of the Monkey but the Chinese New Year began on February 16 so a person born in January or early February 1980 would belong to the year before – the year of the Goat.

And there's more to it than that...

In case you're saying to yourself, but surely, how can every person born in the same 365 days have the same personality(?) – you're quite right. The birth year is only the beginning.

Your birth year reflects the way others see you and your basic characteristics, but your month and time of birth are also ruled by the celestial animals – probably different animals from the one that dominates your birth year. The personalities of these other animals modify and add talents to those you acquired with your birth year creature.

The 1920s

5 February 1924 – 24 January 1925 | RAT

25 January 1925 – 12 February 1926 | OX

13 February 1926 – 1 February 1927 | TIGER

2 February 1927 – 22 January 1928 | RABBIT

23 January 1928 – 9 February 1929 | DRAGON

10 February 1929 – 29 January 1930 | SNAKE

The 1930s

30 January 1930 – 16 February 1931 | HORSE

17 February 1931 – 5 February 1932 | GOAT

6 February 1932 – 25 January 1933 | MONKEY

26 January 1933 – 13 February 1934 | ROOSTER

14 February 1934 – 3 February 1935 | DOG

4 February 1935 – 23 January 1936 | PIG

24 January 1936 – 10 February 1937 | RAT

11 February 1937 – 30 January 1938 | OX

31 January 1938 – 18 February 1939 | TIGER

19 February 1939 – 7 February 1940 | RABBIT

The 1940s

8 February 1940 – 26 January 1941 | DRAGON

27 January 1941 – 14 February 1942 | SNAKE

15 February 1942 – 4 February 1943 | HORSE

5 February 1943 – 24 January 1944 | GOAT

25 January 1944 – 12 February 1945 | MONKEY

13 February 1945 – 1 February 1946 | ROOSTER

2 February 1946 – 21 January 1947 | DOG

22 January 1947 – 9 February 1948 | PIG

10 February 1948 – 28 January 1949 | RAT

29 January 1949 – 16 February 1950 | OX

The 1950s

17 February 1950 – 5 February 1951 | TIGER

6 February 1951 – 26 January 1952 | RABBIT

27 January 1952 – 13 February 1953 | DRAGON

14 February 1953 – 2 February 1954 | SNAKE

3 February 1954 – 23 January 1955 | HORSE

24 January 1955 – 11 February 1956 | GOAT

12 February 1956 – 30 January 1957 | MONKEY

31 January 1957 – 17 February 1958 | ROOSTER

18 February 1958 – 7 February 1959 | DOG

8 February 1959 – 27 January 1960 | PIG

The 1960s

28 January 1960 – 14 February 1961 | RAT

15 February 1961 – 4 February 1962 | OX

5 February 1962 – 24 January 1963 | TIGER

25 January 1963 – 12 February 1964 | RABBIT

13 February 1964 – 1 February 1965 | DRAGON

2 February 1965 – 20 January 1966 | SNAKE

21 January 1966 – 8 February 1967 | HORSE

9 February 1967 – 29 January 1968 | GOAT

30 January 1968 – 16 February 1969 | MONKEY

17 February 1969 – 5 February 1970 | ROOSTER

The 1970s

6 February 1970 – 26 January 1971 | DOG

27 January 1971 – 14 February 1972 | PIG

15 February 1972 – 2 February 1973 | RAT

3 February 1973 – 22 January 1974 | OX

23 January 1974 – 10 February 1975 | TIGER

11 February 1975 – 30 January 1976 | RABBIT

31 January 1976 – 17 February 1977 | DRAGON

18 February 1977 – 6 February 1978 | SNAKE

7 February 1978 – 27 January 1979 | HORSE

28 January 1979 – 15 February 1980 | GOAT

The 1980s

16 February 1980 – 4 February 1981 | MONKEY

5 February 1981 – 24 January 1982 | ROOSTER

25 January 1982 – 12 February 1983 | DOG

13 February 1983 – 1 February 1984 | PIG

2 February 1984 – 19 February 1985 | RAT

20 February 1985 – 8 February 1986 | OX

9 February 1986 – 28 January 1987 | TIGER

29 January 1987 – 16 February 1988 | RABBIT

17 February 1988 – 5 February 1989 | DRAGON

6 February 1989 – 26 January 1990 | SNAKE

The 1990s

27 January 1990 – 14 February 1991 | HORSE

15 February 1991 – 3 February 1992 | GOAT

4 February 1992 – 22 January 1993 | MONKEY

23 January 1993 – 9 February 1994 | ROOSTER

10 February 1994 – 30 January 1995 | DOG

31 January 1995 – 18 February 1996 | PIG

19 February 1996 – 7 February 1997 | RAT

8 February 1997 – 27 January 1998 | OX

28 January 1998 – 5 February 1999 | TIGER

6 February 1999 – 4 February 2000 | RABBIT

The 2000s

5 February 2000 – 23 January 2001 | DRAGON

24 January 2001 – 11 February 2002 | SNAKE

12 February 2002 – 31 January 2003 | HORSE

1 February 2003 – 21 January 2004 | GOAT

22 January 2004 – 8 February 2005 | MONKEY

9 February 2005 – 28 January 2006 | ROOSTER

29 January 2006 – 17 February 2007 | DOG

18 February 2007 – 6 February 2008 | PIG

7 February 2008 – 25 January 2009 | RAT

26 January 2009 – 13 February 2010 | OX

The 2010s

14 February 2010 – 2 February 2011 | TIGER

3 February 2011 – 22 January 2012 | RABBIT

23 January 2012 – 9 February 2013 | DRAGON

10 February 2013 – 30 January 2014 | SNAKE

31 January 2014 – 18 February 2015 | HORSE

19 February 2015 – 7 February 2016 | GOAT

8 February 2016 – 27 January 2017 | MONKEY

28 January 2017 – 15 February 2018 | ROOSTER

16 February 2018 – 4 February 2019 | DOG

5 February 2019 – 24 January 2020 | PIG

The 2020s

25 January 2020 – 11 February 2021 | RAT

12 February 2021 – 31 January 2022 | OX

1 February 2022 – 21 January 2023 | TIGER

22 January 2023 – 9 February 2024 | RABBIT

10 February 2024 – 28 January 2025 | DRAGON

29 January 2025 – 16 February 2026 | SNAKE

17 February 2026 – 5 February 2027 | HORSE

6 February 2027 – 25 January 2028 | GOAT

26 January 2028 – 12 February 2029 | MONKEY

13 February 2029 – 2 February 2030 | ROOSTER

CHAPTER 2: THE RAT

Rat Years

5 February 1924 – 24 January 1925

24 January 1936 – 10 February 1937

10 February 1948 – 28 January 1949

28 January 1960 – 14 February 1961

15 February 1972 – 2 February 1973

2 February 1984 – 19 February 1985

19 February 1996 – 7 February 1997

7 February 2008 – 25 January 2009

25 January 2020 – 11 February 2021

Natural Element: Water

It may seem strange to start the astrological cycle with such a controversial creature as the Rat. Here in the West, the Rat has a serious PR problem. We just don't like rats. We hear about 'plagues' of rats, they 'infest' dirty, derelict places, and they hang around dustbins. They're associated with disease, rubbish, and sewers, and if a rat should be spied near our homes, we'd be straight on the phone to pest control. Describe a person as 'a rat' and you're certainly not paying them a compliment.

Yet the Chinese view things differently. They may not exactly welcome a feral rodent into their house, but they recognise many admirable qualities in the species. Rats are great survivors; they're quick, intelligent, tenacious, and they seem to thrive almost anywhere, under any conditions. All excellent qualities to be commended, if you happen to be human.

So, far from being an unfortunate sign, being born in the year of the Rat is regarded as a good omen.

Rats possess great charm and elegance. They're chatty, intelligent, and make friends easily. At parties, people seem drawn to them. There's something about their genuine enjoyment of being surrounded by new faces that makes them easy to get along with. Yet, they value old friends too, will make an effort to stay in touch, and a friendship with a rat is likely to last a lifetime.

Both male and female rats always look good. They believe that outward appearances are important. Instinctively, they understand that you only get one chance to make a first impression, so they take care never to be caught off guard looking a mess.

This happy knack is easier for them than most because they love shopping and are Olympic-standard bargain hunters. They can't resist a sale and if it's a designer outlet so much the better. Their homes are usually equally smart for the same reason. Rats have innate good taste and are as thrilled with finding a stylish chair or piece of artwork at half price as they are a pair of shoes.

They enjoy spending money and the challenge of hunting down the best deal, and because they're also successful at work, they tend to have plenty of cash to splurge. Yet, despite this, Rats can often be viewed as a bit stingy. They're not mean, it's just that Rats' strong survival instincts lead them to prioritise themselves and their family when it comes to allocating their resources. Within their families, Rats are extremely generous.

Rats also enjoy the finer things in life. They prefer not to get their hands dirty if at all possible and are experts at getting other people to do the mundane tasks for them. They like pampering and luxury and lavish holidays. Yet, being supremely adaptable, they will happily embark on a backpacking trip if it takes them where they want to go and there's no other option. They're adventurous, and hate to be bored, so they're prepared to take a calculated risk if some place or person catches their eye.

Yet, this willingness to take a risk combined with the love of a bargain can occasionally get them into trouble, despite their super-sensitive survival instincts. Rats, particularly male Rats, have to guard against the urge to gamble. The combination of the prospect of winning easy money, the excitement of the element of chance, and the challenge of pitting their wits against the odds can prove irresistible. What starts as a mild flirtation for fun can end up as quite a problem.

The same could be said for suspect 'get-rich-quick' schemes. Though clever and sceptical enough to see through them, Rats are so thrilled by the idea of an easy gain, the temptation to cast doubts aside, against their better judgement, can be overwhelming.

But if any sign can get away with such unwise habits, it's probably the Rat. Rats are good at making money and at handling money. They're also masters at spotting an escape route and scuttling away down it if the going gets too tough. Underneath that gregarious bonhomie, there's a shrewd, observant brain that misses nothing. Rats have very sharp eyes and are highly observant even when they don't appear to be taking any notice. They are also very ambitious, though they tend to keep it quiet. Dazzled by their genuine charm and witty conversation, people often fail to see that most moves Rats make are taking them methodically to the top. It's no accident they call it 'the rat race'.

Best Jobs for Rats

Financial Consultant

Mortgage Advisor

Lawyer

Private Detective

Manager of any kind

Sales of Luxury Items

Perfect Partners

Cupid's arrow can strike anywhere at any time, of course, but once the novelty of new romance wears off, some relationships are easier to maintain than others. Here's a guide to the Rat's compatibility with other signs.

Rat with Rat

These two are certainly on the same wavelength and share many interests. When their eyes first meet, passionate sparks may fly. This relationship could work very well, though over time the competitive and ambitious nature of both partners could see them pulling in different directions. What's more, if one should succumb to a weakness for gambling or risky business ventures while the other does not, it will end in tears.

Rat with Ox

Oddly enough, this combination can be surprisingly successful. Frenetic Rat and calm Ox may seem to be opposites but, in fact, Rat can find Ox's laid-back approach strangely soothing. Ox is not interested in competing with Rat and will put up with Rat's scurrying after new schemes with patience. As long as Rat doesn't get bored and has enough excitement in other areas of life, this relationship could be very contented.

Rat with Tiger

The magnificent Tiger will always catch Rat's eye because Rat loves beautiful things, but Tiger's natural element is fire and Rat's is water and fire and water don't mix well. Tiger's not interested in Rat's latest bargain, and Rat doesn't share Tiger's passion for changing the world, yet the attraction is strong. If Rat makes an effort to step back and not get in Tiger's way, they could reach a good understanding.

Rat with Rabbit

Rat finds Rabbit intriguing. Here is an attractive, stylish creature that doesn't feel the need to be pushy or take centre stage yet somehow manages to be at the heart of things. The Rat wants to find out more, while Rabbit is flattered and entertained by witty Rat's attention. These two respect each other but, over the long-term, Rat could be too overpowering.

Rat with Dragon

This couple is usually regarded as a very good match. They have much in common being action-loving, excitement-seeking personalities who hate to be bored. It takes a lot to dazzle Rat, but the Dragon's glamorous aura proves irresistible, while Dragon loves to be admired, so each enjoys being with the other. There could be the odd power struggle as these two are both strong characters, but the magnetism is so powerful they usually kiss and make up.

Rat with Snake

The Snake shares Rat's good taste and being elegant, sophisticated, and smart will delight Rat at first sight. These two get on very well on an intellectual level but perhaps are better as good friends rather than long-term partners. The Snake's love of basking in the sun for hours strikes

Rat as lazy and dull, while Rat's need to rush around doing deals and meeting people seems pointless and wearying to the Snake.

Rat with Horse

Rat and Horse both fizz with energy and they love action and looking good, yet this is not seen as an ideal partnership. Nothing's impossible, of course, but these two will have to work hard to find harmony. The Rat will admire Horse's enthusiasm and cheerful approach but become impatient to discover Horse can also be fiery and emotional. Horse, on the other hand, can find Rat's risk-taking behaviour extremely worrying.

Rat with Goat

The Rat is charmed by carefree Goat and fascinated by its artistic talent and happy knack of living in the present. Easy-going Goat tends to like everyone so is perfectly content to enjoy Rat's company. These two can get along fine, yet they don't really understand each other deep down. Long-term, the Rat may find Goat's lack of interest in the practical side of life, such as finances and bills, irritating.

Rat with Monkey

Unlikely as it might appear, mischievous Monkey and the clever Rat make a good partnership. Their quick minds, sociable natures, and love of novelty ensure that they're never bored together. True, Rat might sometimes feel Monkey is too inclined to skim over the surface of things and could do with being more serious at times, but Monkey's ingenuity and audaciousness always save the day. Both can have a weakness for gambling though, so need to take care.

Rat with Rooster

The first thing Rat notices about the Rooster is its beautiful plumage, but this a relationship which is unlikely to get much further than initial admiration. Rooster's direct and frank approach can strike the Rat as tactless, while the Rooster can't understand why Rat has to make life so convoluted and complicated. Then again, Rooster's natural confidence and aplomb can come across as bragging to the Rat. These two have to be very determined to make a partnership work.

Rat with Dog

The Rat and the Dog get along pretty well together. Both are strong characters, and they respect each other and give each other space when required. But deep down, the Dog is a worrier and gets anxious about unnecessary risks, while Rat just can't help sailing close to the wind if an interesting opportunity presents itself. Long-term, reckless Rat might unintentionally drive Dog to distraction. Only to be considered by Dogs with nerves of steel.

Rat with Pig

It's very easy for Rat to be beguiled by the Pig. Pig's easy-going, sympathetic nature immediately relaxes the Rat. What's more, Pig loves shopping as much as Rat so the two of them could enjoy many happy expeditions together. Conflict could occur through overspending. Pig does not understand Rat's compulsion to bag a bargain. Pig will buy at whatever the price and the two could end up arguing over money.

Success For the Rat in The Year of the Pig

2019 looks like being an excellent year for Rats everywhere. The easy-going Pig gets along with most of the creatures in the zodiac, and the Rat is no exception. Yet the Rat's year will turn out subtly different, in tone, to the twelve months experienced by their fellow zodiac animals.

Instinctively, Rats sense that the era they ushered in twelve years ago is coming to an end and very soon, they'll be called upon to lead the pack into the next twelve-year cycle.

Those sensitive Rat whiskers are picking up hints of an exciting change in the wind. A change of course. Yet, right now, they've got to concentrate on tying up a thousand loose ends. This is a year for clearing the clutter from every facet of the Rat life – for finishing all those uncompleted projects – so they can emerge lean and fit and ready to spring into action in 2020.

While Rats are longing for a big change, 2019 is about daydreaming, and planning, and looking back over the past twelve years to see what worked well and what it is time to jettison. Suddenly, they see where big improvements can be made and where fabulous opportunities can be found. But it wouldn't be wise to rush in yet. This year, Rats have the luxury of time to research, organise, and refine those plans, and next year the wisdom of this approach will become dazzlingly obvious.

It's not a waste of time for Rats to dream and dream big in 2019 because the seeds sown now will come to fruition, gloriously, in the next few years. What's more, Rats can afford to take some time out now, as the rewards for past efforts are starting to flow in. The Pig will bring Rat plenty of cash but, also, plenty of opportunities to spend it as well; so don't go crazy!

This isn't an ideal year to change careers, but ambitious Rats could find themselves in line for a promotion in their existing job, in recognition of previous hard work. The emphasis is on reward for what's gone before so Rats who earn commission, royalties, or dividends will enjoy a boost to their finances and student Rats – who've been studying conscientiously – should be successful in their exams.

For the same reason, this is not the perfect year to move house (although if it's essential, it can't be helped) though it would be an excellent time to house hunt, explore new areas, and possibly check out some completely different lifestyles because who knows where and how you might prefer to live in the coming era? For now, restless Rats who'd like a change could use some of that extra cash to splash out on exciting home improvements.

Certainly, since the Earth element of 2019 encourages acts of kindness to others, it would be a particularly auspicious move this year to parcel up as many little-used possessions as possible and donate them to a charity shop – which will also free up your home for the changes to come.

As the year progresses and Rats cast a critical eye over the areas of their lives that could work better, they may decide it's time to slip away from certain relationships and associations that no longer seem beneficial. There's no need for dramatic gestures. If certain people in the Rat circle have become hard work or cause Rats to feel bad for any reason, this is the ideal moment to quietly see less and less of them until they've faded out altogether. The Year of the Pig encourages every kind of clutter-clearing for Rats, so human energy-vampires should be top of the list to go.

Before 2019 is out, you're likely to have waved goodbye to a number of individuals from whom you've grown apart – even if they haven't realised it yet!

But Rats that end up pruning their acquaintances this year have no need to fear being lonely. The Year of the Pig brings endless opportunities for socialising. Rats love a party, and this will be a sparkling twelve months of celebrations and get-togethers. What's more, since gregarious Rats can't help mixing business with pleasure, the chances are that new friends made this year will lead to unexpected opportunities in 2020 and beyond.

Love

The good news is that Rats will enjoy more than their fair share of romance this year. Single Rats could find though, that while new relationships will be great fun, they're unlikely to last forever. If you haven't yet met your soulmate, 2019 is probably not the year they'll turn up. On the other hand, there'll be plenty of contenders to audition for the role while you wait for Mr or Ms Right. Watch out for complications while you pick and choose though. Rats could find themselves accidentally entangled with partners who're not as free as they might suggest.

Rats already in relationships should have a happy twelve months if they steer clear of disagreements about money. This year's compulsion to spend could lead to problems. Also, although settled Rats may not be planning to change, an unexpected temptation could occur. A chance meeting with a stranger or an incident at work that throws you together with a colleague could lead to tricky repercussions. Resist if you want your relationship to last.

Keys to Success

The most difficult aspect of this promising year for the Rat is the need for patience. Everything is going well. Rats don't have to exert themselves too much to achieve their aims, and finances will be fine as long as Rat does nothing rash. Yet, Rats are always in a hurry. It's quite stressful for the Rat to be forced to relax, and lazing around enjoying the good life doesn't come naturally. Rat's need for action and constant mental stimulation could lead to risky behaviour in 2019. Gambling, rash speculation – particularly with property and unwise love tangles – could ruin an otherwise lucky year. Count to ten before leaping into the unknown (and preferably decide against it); learn to sit back and put your feet up a bit, and this will be a delightful year.

The Rat Year at a Glance

January – Everything seems to be under control. You're keen to tackle your to-do list.

February – You hear news of wedding bells and possibly a baby's on the way. Just don't let the excitement make you careless. Accidents could happen.

March – A project leads to success. Crack open the champagne.

April – There's still cause for celebration. Partying and socialising are fun; take care not to over-indulge.

May – It might be spring, but you could do with easing up.

June – You're drawn to training of some kind to further your career or future prospects. Improve your skills and luck will follow.

July – Sexy vibes are distracting this month. Don't be thrown off course.

August – The perfect time to take a holiday and get in shape.

September – Your career is looking up. You're getting noticed.

October – As the nights draw in, avoid coughs and colds – you're susceptible to bugs this month.

November – The pace is increasing. Everything you do seems to go well.

December – One of your best months. At work you're flavour of the month and along comes romance linked with travel. Enjoy.

Lucky Colours for 2019: Sage green, pink and golden yellow

Lucky Numbers for 2019: 2, 3

CHAPTER 3: THE OX

Ox Years

25 January 1925 – 12 February 1926

11 February 1937 – 30 January 1938

29 January 1949 – 16 February 1950

15 February 1961 – 4 February 1962

3 February 1973 – 22 January 1974

20 February 1985 – 8 February 1986

8 February 1997 – 27 January 1998

26 January 2009 – 13 February 2010

12 February 2021 – 31 January 2022

Natural Element: Water

It's probably quite difficult for us in the West to picture an Ox. We might encounter cows and the odd scary bull on a country walk but oxen haven't been part of our rural scene for centuries.

Yet once, they were an essential feature of farm life – with teams of oxen patiently pulling the plough across the fields where now there are only tractors. Perhaps they're still in use in China, but whether they are or not, the Ox has long been revered there. No village was complete without its team of oxen and traditionally the Chinese didn't eat beef (though many do these days) because the ox was regarded as a gift from the Gods - so vital to country folk they couldn't possibly disrespect the beast by serving it up for dinner.

So while the Ox may not seem as glamorous as some of the other celestial animals, the sign of the Ox is respected and appreciated.

The Ox has phenomenal strength and endurance. Get an Ox moving and it will plod on mile after mile, covering huge distances with apparent ease and without complaint. For this reason, Ox's often end up being very successful in whatever they undertake – from their career to their favourite hobby or creating a family that blossoms.

They have a wonderful knack of planning a sensible, logical course to wherever they want to go and then following it, relentlessly, step by step until they get there, no matter what obstacles they encounter en route. Ox's find it rather puzzling that other people can't seem to adopt the same simple approach. They don't understand why some signs give up before reaching their goal. Why do they waste their time chopping and changing and getting nowhere, wonders the Ox.

Ox patience is legendary. They may not be quick, or nimble but they realise slow, steady, consistent effort achieves far more in the long run. And the Ox is only interested in the long haul. At heart, the Ox is serious minded and though they enjoy a joke as much as anyone else, they regard frivolity as a pleasant diversion, not an end in itself.

Ox people are usually good-looking in a healthy, wholesome way but they're not impressed by flashy, passing whims and fashions. Superficial gloss has no appeal. The Ox woman is unlikely to be found rocking extreme, designer clothes or wafting fingers iridescent with the latest nail polish.

Ox tastes tend to be classic and practical. They are instinctively private and hate to draw attention to themselves, yet the Ox is one of the nicest signs. Genuinely honest, kind and sincere, Ox is ready to help anyone in trouble, happily pitching in to lend a hand without expecting anything in return. Yet since Ox tends to speak only when they have something to say, other signs can find them difficult to get to know. It's worthwhile making the effort because the Ox will be a loyal friend forever.

What's more, when they do have something to say Ox views can be surprisingly frank. Just because they are patient and kind it doesn't mean they can be pushed around. The Ox is self reliant and makes up its own mind, it's not swayed by the opinions of others. What's more they can be very stubborn. When the Ox finally makes a decision, it sees no reason to change it.

Ox people are not materialistic. They work hard because the task interests them or because they can see it needs to be done and they will keep going until the project is complete. They are the true craftsmen of the zodiac, excelling in working with their hands and they can be unexpectedly artistic and innovative when the occasion demands. As a result money can accumulate and Ox is not averse to spending it on some creature comforts. The Ox home will be warm and styled for comfort and practicality rather than cutting-edge design. If there's no space for a garden it's likely to be filled with houseplants too because Ox has green fingers and needs to see nature close at hand.

Travel and holidays are not top of the Ox agenda; they enjoy their work and their home and are not forever itching to get away. Unlike many signs they cope with routine very well. And for all their modesty and quiet diligence there is always something impressive about the Ox. Other signs sense the latent strength and power that lies just below the surface and tend not to impose too much. This is just as well because though the Ox may appear calm, placid and slow to anger, when they do finally lose their temper, it can be terrifying. What's more, the Ox will never forget an insult and can bear a grudge for years. Ox doesn't stay mad – they get even.

Best Jobs for Ox

Farmer

Horticulture; florist, gardener, botanist

garden designer

Medical Worker

Carer

Solicitor

Accountant

Potter or craft worker of some kind

Soldier

Teacher

Perfect Partners

Cupid's arrow can strike anywhere at any time, of course, but once the novelty of new romance wears off, some relationships are easier to maintain than others. Here's a guide to the Ox's compatibility with other signs.

Ox with Ox

These two could be very happy together, as long as one of them plucks up the courage to admit they're interested. Sloppy, sentimental romance is not their style and they both share this view so there'll be no misunderstandings around Valentine's Day. They know that still waters run deep and they can enjoy great contentment without showy declarations of love.

Ox with Tiger

Not an easy match. Ox and Tiger could be on different planets. Fiery Tiger doesn't frighten Ox and Tiger may admire Ox's strong, good looks and sincere nature but they both need different things from life. Tiger wants to dash about changing the world for the better, while Ox reckons you get more done by buckling down where you happen to be and attending to the details. Clashes could abound.

Ox with Rabbit

Ox finds Rabbit rather cute and appealing. Whether male or female there's something about Rabbit's inner fluffiness that brings out Ox's highly developed protective instincts. Rabbit meanwhile loves the Ox's reassuring presence and the sense of security Ox provides. These two could get on very well together as long as refined Rabbit can overlook Ox's occasional down-to-earth — Rabbit might say 'coarse' - observations.

Ox with Dragon

Chalk and cheese though this pair may appear to be there's a certain fascination between them. Ox may not approve of Dragon's showy manner but recognises Dragon's good intentions, while Dragon admires Ox's strength of character and gift for completing tasks. If each could find a way to tolerate the other's wildly different lifestyles, they might be good for each other, but long term, Dragon's hectic pace might wear even the Ox's legendary stamina.

Ox with Snake

Like Ox, the Snake is quietly ambitious and not given to racing around unless it's absolutely necessary. Ox on the other hand respects Snake's clever brain and understated elegance. These two could quickly discover how beneficial an alliance between them would be. They're both happy to give the other space when required but also step in with support when needed. This could be a very successful match.

Ox with Horse

Long ago on many Western farms, Ox was replaced by the Horse and it maybe that Ox has never forgotten and never forgiven. At any rate, these two, despite both being big, strong animals are not usually friends. Horse is too flighty and frivolous to interest Ox for long, while Ox's methodical, careful ways will irritate the Horse. Best not to go there.

Ox with Goat

Though these two share artistic natures even if in the case of the Ox, they're well hidden, deep down they don't 'get' one another. Ox may be beguiled at first by Goat's friendly, easy-going manner but then disappointed to discover Goat seems to find everyone equally delightful, even those who're plainly unworthy. Goat on the other hand can't understand why Ox won't lighten up more. This relationship would require a lot of effort and compromise.

Ox with Monkey

The naughty Monkey scandalises Ox but in such an amusing way Ox can't help laughing. Monkey on the other hand is equally amused to find an audience so easy to shock. This unlikely pair enjoy each other's company and get on surprisingly well. Yet right from the start it's probably obvious to both that a long term relationship couldn't last. A fun flirtation though could be a terrific tonic for them both.

Ox with Rooster

For all its bravado and showing off, the Rooster is a down-to-earth type, drawn to security and accumulating the good things in life – requirements that Ox understands very well and can supply effortlessly. What's more, Ox can't help but admire Rooster's fine feathers and skill at communicating in a crowd – attributes Ox doesn't have and is unlikely to acquire. These two could enjoy a very good partnership.

Ox with Dog

These two ought to get along well as they're both sensible, down to earth, loyal and hard working and in tune with each other's basic beliefs. And yet, somehow they don't. Dog has a playful streak and finds this lacking in Ox, while Ox may be baffled by what seems like pointless silliness in Dog. If they can agree to differ they could make a relationship work.

Ox with Pig

Delightful Pig will catch Ox's eye and since Pig isn't a constant thrill-seeker, the two of them could enjoy many peaceful evenings together perhaps over a tasty meal. Yet Pig's spendthrift ways – at least in Ox's eyes, could soon prove very annoying as well as illogical to the Ox, while Pig could find Ox's attitude judgemental and upsetting. Not ideal for the long term.

Ox with Rat

Oddly enough, this combination can be surprisingly successful. Frenetic Rat and calm Ox may seem to be opposites, but in fact Rat can find Ox's laid-back approach strangely soothing. Ox is not interested in competing with Rat and will patiently put up with Rat's scurrying after new schemes. As long as Rat doesn't get bored and generates enough excitement in other areas of life, this relationship could be very contented.

Success For the Ox in The Year of the Pig

The great thing about the Ox and the Pig is that they're both farmyard animals and they both belong to the water family of zodiac creatures. This means they have a lot in common even though they don't always see eye to eye on everything. So, overall, 2019 looks like being a good year for the Ox.

True, on the face of it, hard-working Ox might not be expected to approve of Pig's hedonistic ways, but even the Ox is wise enough to see that a sensible work-life balance is in everyone's interests. This year, the Ox will be presented with more opportunities to enjoy a break than usual and, for once, Ox might even agree to take them.

It looks as if travel in one form or another will be very much on the Ox's agenda in 2019, even if (at the moment) there's nothing planned. These trips may be connected to career and may well crop up with little warning, so untypical Oxen who are picky about their clothes and appearance should keep suitcase-friendly outfits close at hand at all times.

Neither the Pig nor the Ox are desperate for long distance journeying, so it's possible the travel will involve a series of shorter, work-related visits; but they're likely to be quite outside the Ox's normal routine.

Most years this might prove unsettling to the Ox, a creature that prefers to be surrounded by familiar scenes, but in 2019 it's different. The Year of the Pig could open with some sort of small disappointment regarding a project begun last year and which appeared to be going smoothly. Some of the zodiac cousins would shrug off such a minor setback and forget about it, but not Ox. Ox has a tendency to brood, and though outwardly modest, Ox is also quietly ambitious too. And stubborn – or as Ox would say, tenacious. Which is often a very good thing and will prove fortunate in 2019.

As Ox repeatedly chews over the circumstances of this disappointment, examining each one in the minutest detail, a different perspective will emerge. After a while, it becomes clear this setback is a blessing in disguise. What's more, Ox could find a solution to the difficulty which leads to spectacular results. Solving this problem is possibly the reason for most of Ox's travel. Or it could be that, as a result of Ox's success, there's a big promotion and more responsibility which in turn leads to the necessity for many trips.

All this is very gratifying and likely to whet Ox's appetite for more success. But, of course, the Year of the Pig is a year of plenty and abundance. So Ox can end up with an abundance of opportunities and work. This is good news and not so good news since Ox has strong workaholic tendencies and could attempt to take on far more than even the legendary Ox stamina can handle.

This is where the need for yet more travelling could arise as Ox is advised to relax and do something soothing to recharge.

There's also a strong possibility this year of a financial boost, yet this isn't necessarily connected with Ox's regular job. An investment, a win of some sort, or even an inheritance could be filling the Ox bank account in a very pleasing way. What's more, perhaps on one of those restful breaks, many Ox types will have time to discover some creative talent they didn't realise they possessed. This talent could lead to big rewards in the years to come.

Yet, with so many good things going on, it seems that in 2019, modest, often overlooked Ox has attracted attention and not all of it welcome. There's a sense of jealousy in the air. Treacherous colleagues or envious rivals could be plotting behind Ox's back. Careful Ox is likely to outwit them though.

Love

If the single Ox can leave work long enough to get out and about, this is an excellent year for romance. In fact, 2019 could be the year the uncommitted Ox finds true love. This is even more likely if Ox can be persuaded to make the first move. Not an easy task because Ox is actually quite shy and finds it very difficult to speak up in non-work-related situations. Yet during the Year of the Pig, it's more worthwhile than ever to be bold. Family celebrations, particularly weddings, could prove the perfect settings for the soulmate to appear. And you never know, by the end of the year, another wedding could be on the horizon.

Oxen in settled relationships could enjoy a blissful year. They should take extra care to be tactful, however. The Pig is a highly sensitive creature and easily hurt while Ox is inclined to be blunt. Thoughtless remarks that might have gone unnoticed last year when tough-skinned Dog was in charge will now cause offense in the Year of the Pig. Those Oxen who cultivate a silver tongue and sweet words will be rewarded with passion and if an addition to the family would be welcome, this is the year a new baby could arrive.

Keys to Success

There are so many good things going on, there's a danger Ox could lose a sense of self-preservation. Overwork is the biggest temptation and the greatest danger this year. The Ox is strong but not immortal, so it's particularly important for Oxen to pace themselves. If possible, cut down on responsibilities, allow more time for every task, and build in periods of rest and relaxation, ideally in the open air. Set these rest periods in stone and don't allow anyone to compromise them. And don't forget to take all your holidays. Also, be on the alert for a back-stabbing colleague, but at the same time, don't over-react and alienate everyone. In fact, the Ox that employs a smile and soft words will end the year with far more friends than enemies.

The Ox Year At a glance

January – the kind of month you enjoy, Ox. Plenty to do and very busy.

February – a challenge arises. It's tricky, but suddenly you're inspired. Genius or what?

March – now you're motoring. You've got a plan, and you know where you're going.

April – A sudden windfall. Have you won the lottery or found some treasure in the attic?

May – Looks like you might be forgetting to eat again, Ox. No one's too busy for a meal. Take time out to organise a healthy diet.

June – Someone is trying to deceive you. Should you confront them or ignore their behaviour? Either way, you're on to them.

July – Even more travel than earlier in the year. Don't let things slide at home as a result.

August – Ok, it's the holiday season so why not take a break like everyone else? Nothing major will happen on the work front while you're away.

September – a project needs adjusting but nothing you can't handle.

October – You're not sure if everything's fixed but keep steady and be patient.

November – Patience has paid off. The outlook is promising, and you seem to be more popular than ever.

December – There are rewards to be enjoyed and some new offers coming your way. Romance is sweet.

Lucky Colours for 2019: Blue, Red, White

Lucky Numbers for 2019: 1, 4

CHAPTER 4: THE TIGER

Tiger Years

13 February 1926 – 1 February 1927

31 January 1938 – 18 February 1939

17 February 1950 – 5 February 1951

5 February 1962 – 24 January 1963

23 January 1974 – 10 February 1975

9 February 1986 – 28 January 1987

28 January 1998 – 5 February 1999

14 February 2010 – 2 February 2011

1 February 2022 – 21 January 2023

Natural Element: Wood

Magnificent, powerful, and blessed with a striking, unusual coat, the Tiger creates awe wherever it goes. It's a very popular sign in China where it is regarded as fortunate and noble. Other animals make way for the Tiger, most are terrified of it, and man can't help being entranced by its savage grace. Yet the Tiger doesn't unsheathe those ferocious claws without good reason. Unless it's hungry or feels threatened, if you keep out of the way of the Tiger, the Tiger will keep out of the way of you.

Yet there's something contradictory about this animal. That striped coat – a combination of light and dark – suggests a dual nature. That black and gold colouring doesn't just look beautiful; it also provides remarkable camouflage in the jungles where the Tiger lives. Tiger can melt into the shadows and become completely invisible, only to reappear without warning when least expected, to devastating effect. You never know quite where you are with the Tiger.

People born under this sign tend to attract good luck. They seem to throw themselves into risky situations and escape unscathed where others would come badly unstuck.

Tigers are fearless and restless. They like to be on the move and get bored easily. Wonderfully good looking, Tigers tend to shine in company and enjoy being surrounded by admirers, as they usually are. While perfectly happy in their own company and not craving attention, Tigers are confident and unfazed by a crowd. They take it as quite natural that other signs seek them out and want to hear their opinions.

The Tiger has a magnetic personality and can be highly entertaining, but they're also surprisingly moody – laughing and joking one minute then flying into a rage over almost nothing the next. Despite this, the Tiger is very idealistic. Tiger can see what's wrong with the world and wants to put it right. What's more, courageous Tiger is quite prepared to get out there and put the necessary changes into action. This is the sign of the daring revolutionary. The trouble is, Tigers can become so accustomed to getting away with audacious acts they forget that deep down, they're big cats and cats are said to have only nine lives. Push their luck too far and, sooner or later, Tiger can find it runs out.

Sporty and athletic, Tigers love to travel and when they're young, the typical Tiger is likely to want to be off to see the world. Even older Tigers insist on regular holidays and would happily take a sabbatical or 'adult gap year' if possible. Luxury travel or budget breaks, they don't really care as long as they're going somewhere different. They don't even mind going on their own if necessary as they're independent and self-assured; confident they'll find an interesting companion from time to time along the way if they need one.

Far too individual to be slaves to fashion, Tigers of both sexes still manage to look stylish and original in a pared down, sleek sort of way. They can't be bothered with fiddly, fussy details and they don't need to be because their natural features attract attention effortlessly. Similarly, the Tiger's home is attractive and unusual, full of intriguing objects and trophies Tiger has collected during their adventures.

At work, if they manage to avoid quarrelling with the boss and walking out – a strong possibility as Tigers hate to be told what to do – Tigers tend to rise to the top of whatever field they happen to be in. But contradictory to the end, the Tiger is just as likely to reach the peak of their profession and then resign to try something new. In business, the Tiger can be creative, innovative, and utterly ruthless to competitors.

Best Jobs for Tiger

Running a business

Heading a charity

Actor

Politician

Environmentalist

Military Chief

Barrister

Perfect Partners

Cupid's arrow can strike anywhere at any time, of course, but once the novelty of new romance wears off, some relationships are easier to maintain than others. Here's a guide to the Ox's compatibility with other signs.

Tiger with Tiger

The attraction between these two beautiful people is powerful. They understand each other so well it's almost like looking in a mirror. They both like to walk on the wild side and will enjoy some exciting adventures together but their moody interludes could lead to fierce quarrels. This match could be compulsive but stormy.

Tiger with Rabbit

Surprisingly, the Rabbit is not intimidated by Tiger's dangerous aura and this attitude immediately appeals to Tiger who enjoys a challenge. Rabbit's calm presence and clever way with words keeps Tiger interested, while Rabbit finds Tiger's adventurous tales entertaining. With care, these two could get on well together for years.

Tiger with Dragon

The two biggest personalities in the zodiac would seem bound to clash. After all, these larger than life characters share so many similarities there's a danger they'd compete. Yet a relationship between the Tiger and Dragon often works very well. They understand each other's impulsive natures but they're also different enough to supply the support the other needs. They'd make a formidable power couple.

Tiger with Snake

Not the best of romances. These two are so fundamentally different that any initial attraction is unlikely to last. Snake likes to bask and conserve energy while Tiger wants to leap right in and race about. Tiger takes in the big picture in a glance and is off to the next challenge while Snake likes to pause, delve beneath the surface, and consider. It wouldn't take long before these two annoy each other.

Tiger with Horse

This athletic pair get on pretty well. They both like physical pursuits, testing their strength out of doors or just enjoying the feel of the wind in their hair and the ground under their feet. True, Horse may not quite understand Tiger's plans for world domination but it doesn't really matter. Horse is happy to be loyal to such a charismatic partner. As they're both moody, there could be rows but making up is exciting.

Tiger with Goat

Tiger and Goat don't have a lot in common. While their aims and temperaments are quite different, they are both sociable creatures and Goat wouldn't mind Tiger attracting all the attention when they're out together. Tiger, in return, would appreciate Goat's lack of jealousy and generosity of spirit. Yet long-term they're likely to drift apart as they follow their different interests.

Tiger with Monkey

Tiger can't help being intrigued by sparkling Monkey and Monkey is flattered by such interest. Who wouldn't enjoy being admired by such a fabulous creature? But irrepressible Monkey just can't help teasing and being teased is not a sensation Tiger is familiar with, nor appreciates. Unless the attraction is very strong, these two will wind each other up until they can bear it no longer and part.

Tiger with Rooster

The only feathered creature in the zodiac, the opulence and novelty of Rooster's appearance will draw Tiger like a magnet. What's more, deep down they are both quite serious-minded types so, on one level, they'll have much to share. Yet, despite this, they're not really on the same wavelength and misunderstandings will keep recurring. Could be hard work.

Tiger with Dog

While not exactly opposites, these two are different enough to intrigue each other yet similar enough in basic outlook to get on well. Both Tiger and Dog are idealistic and uninterested in material gain yet where Dog can be nervous, Tiger's bold; and where Tiger attracts controversy, Dog will be loyal. This partnership could be lasting and valuable.

Tiger with Pig

Carefree Pig will love to bask in Tiger's impressive aura, while Tiger will feel good about protecting this charming but unworldly creature. They enjoy each other's company and Tiger, so focused on lofty matters will find Pig's compulsive shopping too trivial to worry about. This couple could do well together as long as Pig's fondness for cosy nights in doesn't make Tiger feel trapped.

Tiger with Rat

Sleek and clever Rat can easily attract Tiger's attention because the intelligent Tiger loves witty conversation. Yet these two are not natural partners. Tiger's not interested in Rat's latest bargain and has no wish to talk about it while Rat doesn't share Tiger's passion for changing the world. Still, if they can agree to step back and not get in each other's way, they could reach a good understanding.

Tiger with Ox

Not an easy match. Ox and Tiger could be on different planets. Fiery Tiger doesn't frighten Ox and Tiger may admire Ox's strong, good looks and sincere nature but they both need different things from life. Tiger wants to dash about creating big changes, while Ox reckons you get more done by buckling down where you happen to be and attending to the details. Clashes could abound.

Success For the Tiger in The Year of the Pig

All the signs suggest that proud Tiger can look forward to a fine year in 2019. Unlikely as it may seem, fierce Tiger and gentle Pig are pretty good friends. What's more, the Tiger is regarded as belonging to the Wood – as in trees and plants – family or element, while the Pig is a Water animal. Wood needs water to grow so, as long as it's not too wet, Wood creatures can flourish when there's water around. And as this year's main element is Earth, this can also be beneficial because few plants can survive without soil.

Last year was also an Earth year, of course, but because it arrived with the Year of the Dog – a strong, masculine energy – and the Tiger is also a strong, masculine energy sign, there could have been a few rows and power struggles along the way. These are much less likely in 2019. The sign of the Pig is a softer, more feminine energy which complements rather than clashes with the strong energy signs. For this reason, Tiger is likely to meet with much more co-operation and agreement than encountered in 2018. People are more likely to say 'yes' to Tiger requests this year.

Yet, delightful as this may sound, it could end up being a bit irritating to the maverick Tiger. Tiger is not a farmyard creature. At heart, the Tiger is still wild, and all this gentle, homely vibe is a bit too domestic for the contrary Tiger taste. Adventurous, thrill-seeking Tiger likes a challenge; prefers to be out there flirting with danger rather than sitting at home by the fireside.

So although this is a good year, the Tiger may have to suppress a certain impatience and settle for smaller-scale adventures. Tigers who manage to conquer their sense of claustrophobia and confinement will be exceptionally successful.

While ambitious, long-distance schemes are not advisable, Tigers could find themselves channelling their need for novelty into moving home or starting a new business. Investments in property are likely to pay off, as is a business connected with catering, food, or any of the delights favoured by zodiac Pigs.

Tigers are born to be self-employed but should they find themselves working for other people, they're likely to do well in their careers this year and could end up with a promotion. This is welcome, but it won't stop restless Tiger from planning an escape into a new venture as soon as possible. Tigers have a very idealistic streak and this year is particularly favoured for any big cats working in the charity sector. For those Tigers who've been thinking about launching a new charity or some sort of voluntary work, this could well be the moment it suddenly comes together and takes off.

Oddly enough, though Tigers are not greatly interested in material possessions, this year they seem to be the recipients of unexpected gifts. Perhaps these are donations to the favoured Tiger charity or maybe more personal. Either way, it's a pleasing development. An increase in income is also likely, though this will come along with an increase in expenditure too, so watch out!

There's a danger too that some sort of novel 'get-rich-quick' scheme will be dangled before the Tiger this year and Tiger will be tempted to suspend disbelief and choose to take the idea at face value. This is probably more out of a desire for excitement than because the project is particularly appealing but whatever the reason, the Tiger should think very carefully before signing anything and take advice. Remember there's no such thing as a free lunch. Down-to-earth ventures, and areas where you have personal expertise and experience, are the favoured fields this year.

Love

Single Tigers are in seductive mood this year. If the bold Tiger spirit can't explore new worlds in 2019, it can certainly be channelled into amorous adventures. Love affairs and new partners could abound. Tiger is never short of admirers but is often too preoccupied to pay them much attention. Now it's different. Forced to remain closer to home, the Tiger suddenly notices the potential and gets creative in love. The flings may not last, but they'll be surprisingly enjoyable. In fact, they may be so enjoyable Tiger may decide to adopt this approach for good.

Attached Tigers have a choice. They can take all that excess energy washing around this year and inject it into their current relationship (carrying it to new heights), or they can cut their losses and move on. Partnerships that have been stumbling along reasonably satisfactorily in years when Tiger is away on Tiger travels for weeks on end, may suddenly collapse when both parties are forced to spend more time together. On the other hand, the relationship could blossom as never before when the couple is finally able to be together. The Tigers who decide to stick around and make the relationship work can unearth delightful discoveries as they explore their joint interests together. Either way, the Tiger benefits.

Keys to Success

The only thing likely to slow you down this year, Tiger, is yourself and your own impatience. Opportunities shower around but at first glance, they're not necessarily the opportunities that excite the picky Tiger. They appear too tame. Yet if the Tiger can overcome an initial lack of interest and delve deeper, unexpected aspects can be found. With patience, these will lead to great success. It's also important to go through unorthodox, untried schemes with a fine toothcomb. Of course, these are exactly the ones that interest Tiger, and in a different year, it might be worth taking a gamble. In 2019, stay on the fence – leave the pioneering to someone else.

The Tiger Year at a Glance

January – This is a lucky year, right, so no need to work too hard? Wrong. You've got the chance to get off to a flying start, so take it.

February – If you put in some extra effort last month, you will begin to see the benefits as early as February. Don't be tempted to exaggerate. You're doing fine as it is. The true situation is good enough.

March – A new project or even a new home is in the offing. Don't rush. Take your time and check the details carefully.

April – Legal issues could arise unexpectedly. Refuse to be drawn into arguments, stay calm and reasonable, and all will be well.

May – Something begun in March is moving forward. Don't let your attention wander. You can make it work with renewed concentration.

June – Summer's here, and you're tempted to head for wide open spaces. Resist. There's still much to do. Patience.

July – People are noticing you more than usual. Maybe they're aware of how well you're doing. Don't strut and preen. Modesty wins friends.

August – Plans are coming to fruition, and the outlook is good. Don't take your eye off the ball at this point.

September – Cash is flowing in. Everyone's happy. If you're longing for a change of scene, this is a good time for a holiday.

October – A minor setback could crop up. Don't be downhearted and don't get angry. Remain calm and reasonable.

November – Back on track. Everything is smoothing over. A little renewed effort should see you where you want to be.

December – Finances are looking good despite the festive season. You can afford to splurge a little and party.

Lucky Colours for 2019: Red, white, beige

Lucky Numbers for 2019: 1, 3, 4

CHAPTER 5: THE RABBIT

Rabbit Years

2 February 1927 – 22 January 1928

19 February 1939 – 7 February 1940

6 February 1951 – 26 January 1952

25 January 1963 – 12 February 1964

11 February 1975 – 30 January 1976

29 January 1987 – 16 February 1988

6 February 1999 – 4 February 2000

3 February 2011 – 22 January 2012

22 January 2023 – 9 February 2024

Natural Element: Wood

Who can resist a rabbit? With their big brown eyes, soft furry bodies, and adorable little bob-tails they can't help but appeal to everyone. Well, almost everyone. If you're a farmer with a field of carrots, or a gardener with a bed of newly planted seedlings, you might not feel so charitable but, in general, rabbits are widely loved, which is why they're the stars of so many cartoons and toy departments.

As a harmless herbivore, the rabbit is a threat to no one. Lacking sharp claws and cruel teeth, rabbits have no means to defend themselves except by running away or freezing still as a stone and hoping to pass for a piece of the undergrowth. What's more, rabbits taste remarkably good to many hungry predators. Given all these apparent disadvantages, you'd think rabbits would have gone the way of the Dodo long ago. Yet quite the opposite. Rabbits are brilliant survivors; despite Myxomatosis, urban development, and global-warming they're still scampering across the fields and congregating on roadside verges at twilight, displaying not a care in the world.

These are tough little creatures, no doubt about it. There's clearly more to the Rabbit than meets the eye – a fact long recognised by the Chinese. It's no accident that in the Chinese calendar, the defenceless, non-swimming Rabbit still manages to cross the river in fourth place, way ahead of stronger, abler creatures with seemingly much more going for them.

People born under this sign are never flashy or loud. Enter a crowded room and the Rabbit wouldn't be the first person you notice. Yet, after a while, a stylish, immaculately turned-out character would draw your eye. Classy and understated with perfect hair and graceful gestures – the typical Rabbit. This effortlessly polished aura is a gift. A Rabbit can emerge soaked to the skin from a rainstorm in a muddy field and within minutes appear clean, unruffled, and co-ordinated. Even Rabbits don't know how they do it. They're not even aware they are doing it.

Rabbits are refined with cultured tastes. They love beautiful things and art of all kinds, and hate to be surrounded by untidiness and disorder. Harmony is very important to the Rabbit – both visually and emotionally. People born in Rabbit years are sensitive in every way. They hate loud noises, loud voices, heavy traffic, and general ugliness. Quarrels can actually make them ill.

Yet this loathing of discord doesn't mean the Rabbit retires from the world. Rabbits somehow manage to end up near the centre of the action and tend to walk away with what they want, without appearing to have made any visible effort to get it.

Softly-spoken Rabbits are natural diplomats. Discreet and tactful, they can always find the right words, the perfect solutions to keep everybody happy. In fact, their powers of persuasion are so sophisticated that people usually do what Rabbit wants in the belief it's their own idea. This approach is so successful that Rabbit can't understand why other signs resort to argument and challenge when so much more can be achieved through quiet conversation and compromise.

Rabbits tend to be brilliant strategists. When other egos get too distracted, jockeying for position and trying to be in charge for the task in hand, Rabbit deftly assesses the situation and has a plan worked out before the others have even agreed an agenda. Outwardly modest, Rabbits rarely admit to being ambitious so they often end up being underestimated. Yet, privately, Rabbits can be single-minded and determined, even ruthless at times. These qualities, combined with their diplomatic skills and calm efficiency, seem to propel them smoothly to the top of whatever profession they've chosen.

Rabbits love their homes, which naturally are as beautiful and harmonious as they are. Home is a sanctuary and Rabbits take a lot of pleasure in choosing just the right pieces and décor to make their special place perfect but in a comfortable way. Tidiness comes easily to them and they can bring order to chaos quickly and neatly with the minimum of fuss. They enjoy entertaining, preferably small, informal gatherings of good friends and they make wonderful hosts. Since they are such agreeable types, they're popular with everyone and a Rabbit's invitation to dinner is accepted with eagerness.

When life is calm and secure, the Rabbit is perfectly happy to stay in one place. These types are not desperate for novelty though they do enjoy a relaxing holiday. Extreme sports are unlikely to appeal but gentle exercise in beautiful surroundings soothes their nerves, and if they can take in an art gallery or a historic church followed by a delicious meal, they'd be truly contented bunnies.

Best Jobs for Rabbit

Diplomat

Political Advisor

Civil Servant

Beauty Therapist

Interior Designer

Hairstylist

Personal Shopper

Graphic Designer

Antiques business

Perfect Partners

Cupid's arrow can strike anywhere at any time, of course, but once the novelty of new romance wears off, some relationships are easier to maintain than others. Here's a guide to the Rabbit's compatibility with other signs.

Rabbit with Rabbit

These two gorgeous creatures look like they're made for each other. Their relationship will always be calm, peaceful, and unruffled and it goes without saying that their home could grace a glossy magazine. Yet though they never argue, the willingness of both partners to compromise could end up with neither ever quite doing what they want. Ultimately, they may find the spark goes out.

Rabbit with Dragon

Dragon is such a larger than life character Rabbit could feel overwhelmed at times. Also, the Dragon can be rather noisy and over-dramatic which would get on Rabbit's nerves. Yet they each admire the other's good points. If they could live next door to each other instead of under the same roof, a long-term relationship might work.

Rabbit with Snake

This subtle pair could make a good combination. They both understand the value of working behind the scenes and neither has any desire to wear themselves out on endless adventures. They share a love of art, fine things, and quiet pleasures, and they both enjoy an orderly home. These two could settle down very happily together.

Rabbit with Horse

This could be tricky. It's fairly unlikely that Horse and Rabbit would ever end up on a date but if they did, and there was a strong attraction, it could lead to a love/hate relationship. Rabbit's neat and tidy ways would enrage Horse and Horse's unpredictable moods and over-the-top reactions would annoy Rabbit. Soon, Horse is likely to bolt for the hills or Rabbit retreat to its burrow.

Rabbit with Goat

Happy-go-lucky Goat is very appealing to Rabbit, particularly as deep down Rabbit is a bit of a worrier. They're both sociable without needing to be the centre of attention and would be happy to people-watch for hours and then cheerfully compare notes afterwards. Goat is tolerant of Rabbit's need for some regular alone time to recharge too, so this couple could be a successful match.

Rabbit with Monkey

Mercurial Monkey doesn't really 'get' Rabbit. The Monkey can appreciate how well Rabbit operates and sees this approach gets good results, but it's all too picky and slow for Monkey. Rabbit, on the other hand, is amused by Monkey's quick wit and clever ways but deplores

Monkey's slapdash, sometimes devious tactics. Very unlikely to work out.

Rabbit with Rooster

Another difficult match. However unfair it seems, Rooster comes over as loud, boastful, and uncouth to Rabbit while Rabbit appears dull, staid, and insufficiently admiring of Rooster's fine feathers to appeal to Rooster. These two just can't see below the surface of the other, and it would be surprising if they ended up together. Only to be considered by the very determined.

Rabbit with Dog

Despite the fact that in the outside world Rabbit could easily end up as Dog's dinner, the astrological pair get on surprisingly well. Dog appreciates Rabbit's careful, efficient ways and soft voice, while Rabbit admires Dog's energy and good intentions. Dog's lack of interest in the finer points of interior design might try Rabbit's patience, but with a little work these two could reach an understanding.

Rabbit with Pig

Pig is not quite as interested in fine dining as Rabbit being as happy to scoff a burger as a Cordon Bleu creation, but their shared love of the good things in life makes these two happy companions. Once again, Pig's spending habits might irritate Rabbit, but not too much as Rabbit is quite willing to splurge on lovely things for the home. A relationship would work well.

Rabbit with Rat

Rat finds Rabbit intriguing. Here is an attractive, stylish creature that doesn't feel the need to be pushy or take centre stage yet somehow manages to be at the heart of things, while Rabbit is flattered and entertained by witty Rat's attention. These two respect each other but long-term, Rat could be too overpowering unless they both agree to give each other space.

Rabbit with Ox

Ox finds Rabbit rather cute and appealing. Whether male or female there's something about Rabbit's inner fluffiness that brings out Ox's highly-developed protective instincts. Rabbit meanwhile loves the Ox's reassuring presence, and the sense of security Ox provides. These two could get on very well together as long as refined Rabbit can overlook Ox's occasional down-to-earth – Rabbit might say 'coarse' – observations.

Rabbit with Tiger

Surprisingly the Rabbit is not intimidated by Tiger's dangerous aura and this attitude immediately appeals to Tiger who enjoys a challenge. Rabbit's calm presence and clever way with words keeps Tiger interested, while Rabbit finds Tiger's adventurous tales entertaining. With care, these two could get on well together for years.

Success For the Rabbit in The Year of the Pig

Lucky Rabbits can look forward to a good time in 2019. Unlike quite a few of the signs, the Rabbits of the zodiac should have been able to navigate the tricky Year of the Dog – 2018 – with comparative ease. Now, the clever Rabbit is set for an even better year in 2019, ruled as it is by the good-natured Pig.

Despite the fact that elegant, sophisticated Rabbit sometimes winces at Pig's less than fastidious ways, this pair actually gets on very well. The Rabbit belongs to the wood family of signs, while the Pig is regarded as a water animal and since water helps wood, in the form of plants and trees, to grow, Rabbits can expect their good fortune to increase in Pig years. What's more, the typical Rabbit is a true, home-loving soul and 2019 is an Earth year – exactly the element that nurtures roots, family, and all matters domestic.

The pace this year will suit Rabbit perfectly. The Earth energy of 2019 is more gentle than last years' and favours slow, steady progress. Get-rich-quick schemes and wild, risky ventures are unlikely to succeed, but that won't bother canny Rabbits. Such vulgarity is just not the Rabbit's style. Projects and ventures that Rabbit has been working on consistently over the months will gradually become more and more successful until, by the end of the year, many a Rabbit will discover, to their delight, they've accumulated quite a substantial amount of cash.

Rabbits involved in artistic, creative, or leisure businesses are likely to do particularly well, and the Pig will reserve a special smile for Rabbits who put their energies into catering.

Oddly enough 2019 is not the ideal year for Rabbits to change jobs. If it's essential to move on then obviously it must happen, but Rabbits attempting to settle down in a new location may find it difficult to feel comfortable, both with their unfamiliar surroundings and with their colleagues. Ideally, the Rabbit will thrive during the next 12 months in a place they know well, where they don't have to divert their energies to getting acclimatised.

Friends will play a big part in the Rabbit's life in 2019. Old friends will grow closer, and new friends could introduce Rabbits to some unusual hobbies or interests which will grow in appeal as the months go on. And, of course, Rabbits who decide to treat their circle to some of their exquisite cooking will find themselves more than usually sought after this year. Eventually, one of these friends could end up enhancing Rabbit's finances in some way. Perhaps they invest in a Rabbit venture, offer valuable advice, or maybe introduce Rabbit to a useful contact. However it happens, friendship will be beneficial to the Rabbit finances.

The domestic vibe of 2019 will encourage many Rabbits to expand or beautify their home. With their bank balances blossoming nicely, this would be a good time for Rabbits to tackle renovations with, of course, kitchen overhauls being particularly favoured. Yet while expanding and improving existing premises is a good idea, actually relocating is not so well starred. Though once again if it's essential then, of course, take a chance.

Love

Single Rabbits may not find their one and only this year, but they won't be short of company. Family occasions and celebrations will be the perfect places for eyes to meet in a pleasing way, and festivities organised by old friends could also lead to romance. These new relationships may not last forever but will be enjoyable nevertheless. Just watch out for jealousy. There could be an atmosphere of competition around love this year. Be on guard against gossip too. A new partner could set tongues wagging.

Committed Rabbits should be ensured a happy year as long as they don't take their partner for granted. The two of you can enjoy spending some of that new found wealth together. What's more, this could be the year Rabbits decide to start a family or add to their existing family. A little piglet in the home would fit in perfectly.

Keys to Success

Much of the fortunate energy for Rabbits this year surrounds career and finances along with slow and steady effort and growth. To make the most of this luck, Rabbits should not allow their attention to be diverted by too much change in other areas. Rabbits are not desperate for pastures new at the best of times so staying put and concentrating is not difficult for them. Keep things tranquil at home, so nothing disturbs the Rabbit peace of mind and success has a fluffy bob-tail.

The Rabbit Year at a Glance

January – You're getting noticed, Rabbit, from day one. Don't let the attention distract you. Keep on doing what you're doing.

February – Things are going well but take care not to spread yourself too thin. You may be asked to take on too many projects. Be selective.

March – Spring is arriving, and your finances are looking up, but don't be too lavish with the spending yet.

April – Competitors appear on the scene. No need to panic. Adopt a calm and discreet manner and carry on.

May – Obstacles recede. Your tactics have paid off. Maintain a steady pace and keep going.

June – Things are going well, and you're about to get a welcome boost. A friend could play an important role.

July – Looks like you've overspent. Don't be downhearted. Spend some time in the open air and nature to help you calm down.

August – A disagreeable person may appear in your orbit this month. Remain polite and patient. They're like that with everyone.

September – Cash is beginning to flow in. Stay prudent. Don't let it go to your head.

October – You may feel like celebrating but take care not to over-indulge. The influence of the Pig could overwhelm Rabbit's usual discipline.

November – Legal issues could demand attention. Read all the small print or take advice.

December – Family fun and celebrations bring joy. Possibly news of a new arrival.

Lucky Colours 2019: Pink, Yellow, Green

Lucky Numbers 2019: 3, 4, 9

CHAPTER 6: THE DRAGON

Dragon Years

23 January 1928 – 9 February 1929

8 February 1940 – 26 January 1941

27 January 1952 – 13 February 1953

13 February 1964 – 1 February 1965

31 January 1976 – 17 February 1977

17 February 1988 – 5 February 1989

5 February 2000 – 23 January 2001

23 January 2012 – 9 February 2013

10 February 2024 – 28 January 2025

Natural Element: Wood

The only mythical creature of the zodiac, the Dragon is undoubtedly the star of the Chinese calendar. Considering it's unlikely these beasts ever existed, it's surprising they're so well known all over the world. Yet they seem to have acquired a split personality. In the West, the Dragon tends to be a villain – swooping on defenceless villages, making off with the prettiest virgins, and incinerating any would-be rescuers with a few puffs of fiery Dragon breath.

In China, on the other hand, the Dragon is revered as a symbol of protection, power, and magnificence. This Dragon is a kindly soul; far from breathing fire, it brought prosperity and rain to parched landscapes. Dragons were always associated with the Emperor and, even today, images of dragons abound throughout the country. No New Year celebration would be complete without the colourful Dragon, dancing through the streets, twisting and turning, and banishing evil spirits as it goes.

'We are descendants of the dragon,' some traditional elders still explain.

The Dragon is regarded as the most fortunate of signs. If at all feasible, Chinese newlyweds try to conceive a Dragon baby. A child born in a Dragon year is believed to bring good luck to the whole family and to this day, the birth rate tends to rise about 5 % in the Chinese community in Dragon years.

There's no doubt the Dragon has huge expectations to live up to. Any other sign could find this intimidating but, fortunately, Dragons are blessed with enormous self-confidence and optimism. The thought that their brilliant reputation could have a downside never even occurs to them.

Dragons tend to dazzle. Even if they're not conventionally good-looking, they stand out in a crowd. They're charismatic with magnetic personalities, formidable energy, and people look up to them. Dragons are so accustomed to attention they rarely question why this should be the case. It just seems like the natural way of the world.

These people think BIG. They're visionaries, bubbling with original new ideas and their enthusiasm is so infectious, their optimism so strong, they easily inspire others. Without even trying, Dragons are born leaders and happily sweep their teams of followers into whatever new venture they've just dreamed up.

The only trouble is, Dragons are easily bored and prefer to rise above trivial matters such as details. With a good second in command, who can attend to the picky minutiae all could be well, but if not, Dragon's schemes can go spectacularly wrong. Yet it hardly seems to matter. The Dragon ascribes to the theory that you have to fail your way to success. Setbacks are quickly forgotten as Dragon launches excitedly into the next adventure and quite often, given the Dragon's good luck, this works.

People born under this sign often enjoy more than their fair share of success and wealth, yet they are not materialistic. They're generous and kind in an absent-minded way and care far more about having a worthy goal than any rewards it might bring. And it is vital for the Dragon to have a goal. A Dragon without a goal is a sad, dispirited creature — restless and grumpy.

Even if it's not large, the Dragon home gives the impression of space and light. Dragons hate to feel confined in any way. They like to look out the window and see lots of sky and have clear, uncluttered surfaces around them even if it's difficult for Dragons to keep them that way.

Yet the Dragon home could have a curiously un-lived in feel. This is because the Dragon regards home as a lair – a comfortable base from which to plan the next project, rather than a place to spend a lot of time.

Dragons love to travel, but they don't really mind where they go as long as it's different and interesting. If they can research a new scheme or cause, en route, so much the better. Yet despite so much going for them, Dragons often feel misunderstood. Their impatience with trivia extends to the irritating need for tact and diplomacy at times. Dragon doesn't get this. If Dragon has something to say, they say it. Why waste time dressing it up in fancy words they think? But then people get upset, and Dragon is baffled. It's not always easy being a Dragon.

Best Jobs for Dragon

Journalist

Politician

Company Director

TV Producer

Explorer

Judge

Inventor

Perfect Partners

Cupid's arrow can strike anywhere at any time, of course, but once the novelty of new romance wears off, some relationships are easier to maintain than others. Here's a guide to the Dragon's compatibility with other signs.

Dragon with Dragon

When Dragon meets Dragon, onlookers tend to take a step back and hold their breath. These two are a combustible mix – they either love each other or loathe each other. They are so alike it could go either way. Both dazzling in their own orbits, they can't fail to notice the other's charms but since they both need to be centre stage, things could get competitive. With give and take and understanding this match could work well, but it won't be easy.

Dragon with Snake

Surprisingly, this couple gets along beautifully. Snake's elegant appearance and quick but subtle mind intrigues Dragon, while Snake admires Dragon's success and endless energy. Snake has no need to battle for the limelight and is quite happy to sit back and support Dragon's schemes from the comfort of a stylish sofa. Which is all the encouragement Dragon needs.

Dragon with Horse

The athletic Horse is pretty good at keeping up with dashing Dragon. And Dragon appreciates a partner who enjoys getting out and about as much as Dragon does. Yet Horse might grow weary of Dragon's constant new projects and resent having to be involved. Horse likes to go off and do Horsey things at frequent intervals which Dragon tends to view as disloyal. This relationship could get fiery.

Dragon with Goat

Goat tends to baffle the busy Dragon. Dragon can see Goat is the creative type but can't understand why Goat doesn't appear to be working very hard when so much could be achieved. In fact, if they stayed together long enough, Dragon could help Goat make the most of many talents, but it's unlikely either of them can sustain enough interest for this to happen.

Dragon with Monkey

These two are likely to hit it off immediately. Each is attracted to the other's intelligence and lively presence, and Dragon's exuberance doesn't overwhelm hyperactive Monkey. What's more, though they both enjoy being surrounded by a crowd, Monkey only wants to make people laugh while Dragon hopes to inspire them to a cause. There is no conflict, so this couple can help each other to go far.

Dragon with Rooster

A Dragon and Rooster pairing will always attract attention. These two are both gorgeous beings and love to be surrounded by admirers. They will probably enjoy going out together and being seen as a couple, but in the long-term, they may not be able to provide the kind of support each secretly needs.

Entertaining for a while but probably not a lasting relationship.

Dragon with Dog

Not the easiest of combinations. Down-to-earth Dog can't see what all the fuss is about when it comes to Dragons. Unimpressed by glamour and irritated by what seems to Dog the gullibility of Dragon admirers, Dog can't be bothered to find out more. Dragon meanwhile is hurt by Dog's lack of interest. Great determination would be needed to make this work.

Dragon with Pig

While Dragon and Pig might seem to be opposites, the two of them can create a surprisingly contented relationship. Pig is quite happy for Dragon to fly around doing exciting things as long as Pig is not expected to do much more than admire profusely. Dragon appreciates Pig's uncritical support and makes allowances for Pig's lack of stamina. This couple could live in harmony.

Dragon with Rat

This couple is usually regarded as a very good match. They have much in common being action loving, excitement-seeking personalities who hate to be bored. It takes a lot to dazzle Rat, but the Dragon's glamorous aura proves irresistible, while Dragon loves to be admired, so each enjoys being with the other. There could be the odd power struggle as these two are both strong characters but the magnetism is so powerful they usually kiss and make up.

Dragon with Ox

Chalk and cheese though this pair may appear to be, there's a certain fascination between them. Ox may not approve of Dragon's showy manner but recognises Dragon's good intentions, while Dragon admires Ox's strength of character and gift for completing tasks. If each could find a way to tolerate the other's wildly different lifestyles, they might be good for each other but, long-term, Dragon's hectic pace might wear down even the Ox's legendary stamina.

Dragon with Tiger

The two biggest personalities in the zodiac would seem bound to clash. After all, these larger than life characters share so many similarities there's a danger they'd compete. Yet a relationship between the Tiger and Dragon often works well. They understand each other's impulsive natures, but they're also different enough to supply the support the other needs. They'd make a formidable power couple.

Dragon with Rabbit

Dragon is such a larger than life character, Rabbit could feel overwhelmed at times. Also, the Dragon can be rather noisy and over-dramatic which would get on Rabbit's nerves. Yet they each admire the other's good points. If they could live next door to each other instead of under the same roof, a long-term relationship might work

Success For the Dragon in The Year of the Pig

Good news Dragon – 2019 looks set to be a far better year than last year. In fact, this year Dragons finally get their sparkle back. Chances are, fire-breathers who are typical of their sign will have found 2018 a bit of a slog. This is because last year was the Year of the Dog, and Dragons and Dogs rarely get on very well.

Both creatures produce strong, powerful energies and – given a level playing field – each is likely to compete for dominance. But in 2018, the playing field wasn't level. It was owned by the Dog, and any powerplay by the Dragon was likely to lead to a nasty clash. Smart Dragons who kept a low profile and quietly and conscientiously persevered with their projects are likely to have done well. But it wouldn't have been easy. It's just not in the Dragon nature to fold its flamboyant wings and melt into the background. Dragons who attempted to carry on as usual will probably have come unstuck.

Happily, all that struggle is now over. 2019 is quite different. The peaceful Pig is too busy looking for fun to wish to dominate Dragon. In fact, Pig rather admires Dragon's radiant charm.

Like the Tiger, the Dragon belongs to the Wood family of growing things and benefits from the nourishing water element that comes with the Pig. This year's earth element can also be helpful to Woods' spreading roots. Nothing's ever perfect, of course. Too much earth can clog water and stop it flowing smoothly, so at times Dragon could get a little bogged down, but overall it's a good year.

Dragons will feel their confidence building as the New Year approaches. Projects begun in 2018 can suddenly leap forward with spectacular results. Dragons who spent the previous 12 months sensibly noting and rectifying previous errors will find their diligence pays off big-time. All at once, hurdles are cleared from their path, past frustrations melt away and Dragons race towards their goal.

In fact, Dragons with the appropriate talents could even find that this is the year when fame and fortune arrives.

Even Dragons who made reasonable progress in their careers or business last year are likely to have felt held back in some way. No longer. Job offers, increased business, and opportunities of every kind will start rolling in. Student Dragons can expect great success in their exams if they cannily put in the hard work last year. Career-minded Dragons will find themselves back in the spotlight, where they know they belong, and their unique qualities receive the attention they deserve.

As with most signs this year, the gentle earth element that permeates the atmosphere favours domestic, smaller-scale, close-to-home endeavours. Dragons like to think big, but in 2019 they'll be less grandiose than usual. There's plenty of scope for travel. In fact, Dragons are likely to be covering a great many miles, particularly in the course of their career, but this is more likely to be made up of frequent shorter trips rather than extended journeys to the other side of the world.

Finances are on the up. Indeed, by the end of the year, Dragons could see substantial gains, possibly as a result of that spectacular success. Pig's spendthrift ways, however, could see more temptations than ever to spend. Having been unusually modest for so long, many Dragons could feel the need to expand into larger, more impressive homes. This could be a good year to move but even though the Dragon bank balance should be healthier in 2019, don't get delusions of grandeur. Remember, rent or a mortgage has to be affordable in bad years as well as good.

Socially, Dragons can look forward to a fabulous 12 months. With confidence restored, the Dragon is back to exuberant, magnificent good form. Last year, possibly without realising it, Dragon tended to hang back. Mixing with others didn't hold its usual appeal. Now, like magic, Dragon's extrovert personality has reappeared along with a host of admirers to appreciate it. Enjoyable parties, get-togethers, celebrations, and even business meetings will boost Dragon's spirits.

Love

Single Dragons will be centre stage once more which is exactly where they like to be.

Surprisingly, given their dashing behaviour, Dragons are not especially keen on mixing and matching partners. Deep down, though they hate to admit it, they are quite vulnerable. They prefer one loyal cheerleader to a succession of flings. This year, unattached Dragons could be delighted to find they meet their soulmate – probably at a social event. Also, for some reason during the coming months, they seem to be strangely attractive to Pigs.

Dragons already involved in a committed relationship could find extra happiness this year. Last year, the stresses and strains caused by the difficult Dog probably soured things a little a home. If the relationship survived, the next few months will see past challenges forgiven and forgotten, and the Dragon and partner can get down to building a contented nest.

Keys to Success

This is a lucky year, Dragon, but the secret to making the most of your good fortune is to be consistent in your efforts and don't allow too much partying to drive you off course. Dragons should also guard against stubbornness. The Pig may be sweet-natured but it has a surprisingly stubborn streak, and this is one area where you could clash. If things aren't going your way, don't dig your heels in, move on. Finally, there's a danger that long-awaited success could go to your head. Obnoxious, boastful Dragons will drive potential allies away. Adopt a modest, grateful air and accept praise gracefully.

The Dragon Year at a Glance

January – Change is in the air. You can sense things are looking up, Dragon. Don't rush. You can afford to take your time.

February – Your career is definitely on the up and a powerful person is taking an interest in you. Turn on the charm.

March – Money rolls in, in a very pleasing way. However, try to resist appeals from family and friends. Wealth can flow out again if you're too generous.

April – Spring is in the air, and you're thinking about romance. An exciting new love interest could appear. Take care if you're already spoken for though.

May – Things are ticking over nicely, but colleagues and acquaintances could be in sensitive mood. Be tactful at all times to avoid inadvertently upsetting anyone.

June – Wedding bells could be ringing – either yours or for someone close. Enjoy the celebrations.

July – This is a good month to take a holiday. You've been working hard, Dragon. Time to rest, relax, and take some gentle exercise.

August – Spirits are high but watch out for a temptation to spend, spend, spend or indulge in risky ventures that involve splashing the cash. They're unlikely to end well.

September – There's a back-to-school feeling but in a good way. You're filled with fresh enthusiasm and new ideas. Follow your heart.

October – Decisions are in the air – possibly to do with career. Restless Dragons may fancy a change of job – but don't jump out of the frying pan into the fire. Consider carefully.

November – October's decisions seem to have paid off, and you're reaping the rewards this month. Unattached Dragons may get a second chance of love.

December – Good luck surrounds you. You may have accumulated wealth if you've avoided the high spending traps. Time to consider how to invest.

Lucky colours for 2019: Gold, Silver, Dove Grey, White

Lucky numbers for 2019: 1, 6, 7

CHAPTER 7: THE SNAKE

Snake Years

10 February 1929 – 29 January 1930

27 January 1941 – 14 February 1942

14 February 1953 – 2 February 1954

2 February 1965 – 20 January 1966

18 February 1977 – 6 February 1978

6 February 1989 – 26 January 1990

24 January 2001 – 11 February 2002

10 February 2013 – 30 January 2014

29 January 2025 – 16 February 2026

Natural Element: Fire

Like the Rat, the Snake tends to have an image problem. In Western eyes, there's not much good to be said about snakes. Ever since the downfall of Adam and Eve, we've held a grudge. Call someone a 'snake in the grass' and it's another way of saying they're treacherous, deceitful, and can't be trusted.

Snakes don't have eyelids which makes their stare disconcerting for a start, they can shed their entire skins which seems downright uncanny, and there's something about the way they slither along without the need for legs that's a bit repellent to a lot of people. It's said that tiny children and animals that have never laid eyes on a snake before will instinctively recoil from a serpent, even though they don't know what it is. Warm and cuddly snakes are not. Some are deadly.

Yet the Chinese hold the Snake in high regard. The Snake is the symbol of wisdom. Even today, in the West, our attitude is ambivalent. The Rod of Asclepius – a snake twisted around a pole – is still a widely used and recognised medical symbol, seen outside pharmacies and doctors' surgeries, even if we don't know that Asclepius was the Greek God associated with healing. And in Greece, in the dim and distant past, snakes were sacred and believed to aid the sick.

So perhaps it's not surprising that in the Chinese zodiac the sign of the Snake is greatly respected. As well as being profoundly wise, the Snake is beautiful – perhaps the most beautiful of all the creatures. Even Snakes who're not born with the most promising features somehow manage to present themselves in such an artful way, they give the illusion of beauty and are admired wherever they go.

The Snake is physically graceful too. Each movement flowing into the next with effortless, elegant economy. Even when they're in a hurry, Snakes appear calm and unrushed and should they arrive late for an appointment they're so charming and plausible with their excuses they're always forgiven.

This is a sign of great intelligence and subtlety. Snakes are never pushy yet can usually slide into the heart of any situation they choose. Their clever conversation and easy charm makes them popular at any gathering. Yet the Snake is picky. Snakes prefer to conserve their energy and don't waste it on activities and people of no interest to them. They are self-contained, quite happy with their own company if necessary, and seldom bored.

At work, Snakes are quietly ambitious, but in line with their policy of conserving energy wherever possible, they will aim for the quickest, easiest route to their goals. Just as the mythical Snake crossed the celestial river wrapped around the hoof of the Horse, the Snake is quite content to link their fortunes to those of a rising star so that Snake is carried to the top in their wake. Ever practical, the Snake has no need for an ego massage – the end result is what matters.

Other signs often mistake Snake's economy of action for laziness, but this is short-sighted. In fact, the Snake is so efficient and so clever that tasks are completed with great speed, leaving Snake with plenty of time to relax afterwards. What's more, in the same way that a snake can shed its skin, people born under this sign are quite capable of suddenly walking out of a situation or way of life that no longer suits them and reinventing themselves elsewhere without a backward glance.

They tend to do this without warning, leaving their previous companions stunned. Only afterwards do people learn that the Snake has been inert and silently brooding for months. But it's no good imploring Snake to return. Snake's actions are swift and irrevocable.

The Snake home is a lovely place. Snakes have perfect taste. They like art, design, good lighting, and comfort. They're excellent hosts. They may not entertain often, unless they can delegate the chores, but when they do, they make it a stylish occasion to remember.

Snakes are known for their love of basking in the sun, and zodiac Snakes are no exception. Trips involving long hikes uphill in the pouring rain will not impress the Snake, but a smart sun-lounger by an infinity pool in a tropical paradise would be Snake's idea of heaven.

People born under this sign have subtle minds fascinated by the unusual and the explained; so books on psychic phenomena, the mysteries of healing, and philosophy could all feature in the Snake's holiday reading.

Best Jobs for Snake

Councillor

Psychiatrist

Doctor

Holistic Therapist

Teacher

Adviser

Psychic Medium

Perfect Partners

Cupid's arrow can strike anywhere at any time, of course, but once the novelty of new romance wears off, some relationships are easier to maintain than others. Here's a guide to the Snake's compatibility with other signs.

Snake with Snake

This fine looking couple turn heads wherever they go. Beautiful and perfectly dressed these two look like the perfect match. They never stop talking and enjoy the same interests so this could be a successful relationship. Long-term, however, there could be friction. They're both experts at getting what they want using the same sophisticated techniques, so they can see through each other.

Snake with Horse

At some level, perhaps, Horse remembers how Snake beat him in the calendar race, so despite an initial attraction, these two could be wary of each other. Snake is impressed by Horse's energy and athleticism while Horse admires Snake's elegance and charm. Yet they don't really have much in common. Deep thinking Snake could find Horse rather shallow and Horse may see Snake as frustratingly enigmatic.

Snake with Goat

Snake and Goat could enjoy many happy hours touring art galleries and exhibitions together. Neither of them craves excitement and harsh, adrenalin-boosting activities, and both appreciate creative artistic personalities. There's no pressure to compete with each other so these two would sail along quite contentedly. Not a passionate alliance but they could be happy.

Snake with Monkey

These two clever creatures ought to admire each other if only for their fine minds and, at first, it's possible they might. But unless they're really determined to make it work, it won't be long before active Monkey finds Snake's energy-saving ways irritating, while Snake loses patience with Monkey's endless jokes.

Snake with Rooster

Surprisingly, Snake and Rooster work well together. Both gorgeous in different ways, they complement each other without competing. Snake's keen eyes can see beneath Rooster's proud facade to the sensitive, unsure person inside, while Rooster appreciates Snake's unobtrusive strength and wise words of encouragement at just the right moment. These two could be inseparable.

Snake with Dog

Some snakes seem to have an almost hypnotic power and, for some reason, Dog is particularly susceptible to these skills. We've heard of snake-charmers but snakes can be dog-charmers and without even trying, Snakes can find themselves the recipients of Dog devotion. Since the Dog is strong, loyal, and can be fun, Snake is not averse to this but might, in the end, find it boring.

Snake with Pig

Pig and Snake don't have a lot to say to each other. Snake can't be bothered with Pig's endless shopping, and Pig is hurt by Snake's snobbish attitude. They both enjoy the good things in life so a luxury fling could briefly be fun – a shared spa break might be a good idea – but in the long-term, this relationship is probably not worth pursuing.

Snake with Rat

The Snake shares Rat's good taste and being elegant, sophisticated, and smart will delight Rat at first sight. These two get on very well on an intellectual level but perhaps are better as good friends rather than long-term partners. The Snake's love of basking in the sun for hours strikes Rat as lazy and dull, while Rat's need to rush around doing deals and meeting people seems pointless and wearying to Snake.

Snake with Ox

Like Ox, the Snake is quietly ambitious and not given to racing around unless it's absolutely necessary. Ox, on the other hand, respects Snake's clever brain and understated elegance. These two could quickly discover how beneficial an alliance between them would be. They're both happy to give the other space when required but also step in with support when needed. This could be a very successful match.

Snake with Tiger

Not the best of romances. These two are so fundamentally different that any initial attraction is unlikely to last. Snake likes to bask and soak up the sun while Tiger wants to explore and discover. Tiger takes in the big picture at a glance and is off to the next challenge while Snake likes to pause, delve beneath the surface, and consider matters. It wouldn't take long before these two annoy each other.

Snake with Rabbit

This subtle pair could make a good combination. They both understand the value of working behind the scenes and neither has any desire to wear themselves out on endless adventures. They share a love of art, fine things, and quiet pleasures and they both enjoy an orderly home. These two could settle down very happily together.

Snake with Dragon

Surprisingly, this couple gets along beautifully. Snake's elegant appearance and quick but subtle mind intrigues Dragon, while Snake admires Dragon's success and endless energy. Snake has no need to battle for the limelight and is quite happy to sit back and support Dragon's schemes from the comfort of a stylish sofa. Which is all the encouragement Dragon needs.

Success For the Snake in The Year of the Pig

Sensuous, sophisticated Snakes can look forward to a year full of opportunities in 2019, but they'll need to employ every ounce of their legendary subtle skills to make the most of them.

The Year of the Pig contains many good things for Snakes, yet the Pig will demand a little more effort and thought on the part of the zodiac Snake, before handing them over, than Snake is accustomed to making. This is because cultured, refined Snake and carefree, sometimes slapdash Pig don't really understand each other deep down. The chic, efficient Snake can find Pig's impetuous, haphazard ways – which occasionally go a bit wrong – irritating, while the Pig ends up offended when sensing serpent criticism.

The Snake belongs to the Fire family of zodiac creatures while the Pig is a water animal – and Fire and Water is not normally a good mix. Snake knows that water could put out serpent fire while Pig's intuitively aware that too much fire could overwhelm the Pig water. It is hardly surprising if these two end up wary of each other.

Yet the cheerful, sweet-natured Pig means no harm to anyone and is quite happy to spread abundance around the zodiac, and the year's Earth energy is supportive of Snakes, so they have a lot going for them.

Career-wise, Snakes will see a number of intriguing offers this year, possibly in areas that Snake has not thought of before. Some of these could be highly unusual, even off the wall ideas, but will be worth exploring. Projects begun last year could also take off and evolve in unexpected but pleasing ways.

The Snake finances are likely to take a turn for the better too; in fact, Snakes could end up in a much healthier condition than they've been for several years.

Along the way, however, Snakes are likely to encounter more than their fair share of obstructive, annoying people. They'll meet plenty of helpful types too, of course, but need to be prepared for the argumentative, disagreeable individuals that will cross the serpent path in 2019.

There could be arguments around the family this year too; yet, there's no need to worry. It seems that some much-needed air-clearing has been building up for quite a while now and once this is out the way, family relationships could be literally transformed. In fact, previously warring members could end up getting on so well together and enjoying each other's company so much, that quite a few Snakes will be inspired to splash out a big chunk of their extra cash on a wonderful family treat of some sort.

Travel is well starred for Snakes in 2019. The accent is on sunshine. The lure of the sun will prove irresistible to Snakes this year, and more than one break to a warm-weather destination is on the cards. Snakes shouldn't stint themselves when the opportunity arises. Frequent basks in the sun will actually boost their luck in 2019.

Love

It may not last, but single Snakes – particularly female serpents – will attract passionate admirers this year. The resulting red-hot dramas could have love/hate overtones but, chances are, Snakes will adore the intrigue. Relationships that survive the hurly-burly – the turbulent splits and the euphoric reconciliations – could well end up becoming permanent commitments.

Settled Snakes may also find their relationship dragged out of a rut in a delightfully unexpected way. If the two of you had been taking each other for granted in the past, this could be the year you start really seeing each other again. In fact, a second honeymoon – somewhere hot of course – would be an excellent idea.

Keys to Success

Snakes like to conserve their energy whenever possible and the temptation this year is to carry on at the same leisurely pace as usual. Yet, this would be a mistake. Snakes can be very successful in 2019, but they need to exert themselves a little bit more. This is not difficult for clever Snakes. It's just that they resent having to bother. Once Snakes have located the right frame of mind, however, they discover it's well worth the effort. Snakes must also be extra patient with all the irritating individuals who cross their paths in the next 12 months. Remember, they can't help not being as well informed as the cultured Snake. A kindly smile and tolerant attitude at all times will work wonders.

The Snake Year at a Glance

January – Great start to the year – you're in such a whirl of activity your feet hardly touch the ground. Exhilarating.

February – Still busy. There's so much to do but make sure you pace yourself. Snakes can run out of stamina. Take plenty of breaks.

March – Crack open the champagne! Looks like some hard work has paid off. A financial boost arrives.

April – Argumentative types surround you. Someone's looking for a fight. Don't rise to the bait.

May – Your special skills are required. Don't rush in, though. Think carefully then act with wisdom.

June – Halfway through the year. You've been working hard. Time to ease up and take a sunshine break.

July – Temptation arrives. Snakes are in restless mood and keen to take a risk that's fun. Gambling and unusual business ventures should be avoided.

August – Your quietly efficient ways are getting noticed. Someone is impressed. Carry on doing what you're doing and adopt a modest expression.

September – Finances are improving. A pay rise is possible. Save as big a chunk as possible.

October – Pressures to spend abound. Resist them if you can. If not, look for discounts and bargains. Do not pay the full price.

November – Good news arrives. Something you've been planning suddenly leaps ahead in the best possible way.

December – Family fortunes are blossoming. Maybe this is the time you decide to spoil them with a big treat.

Lucky colours 2019: Green, silver, Yellow

Lucky Numbers 2019: 2, 8, 9

CHAPTER 8: THE HORSE

Horse Years

30 January 1930 – 16 February 1931

15 February 1942 – 4 February 1943

3 February 1954 – 23 January 1955

21 January 1966 – 8 February 1967

7 February 1978 – 27 January 1979

27 January 1990 – 14 February 1991

12 February 2002 – 31 January 2003

31 January 2014 – 18 February 2015

17 February 2026 – 5 February 2027

Natural Element: Fire

Though traditionally the Dog is supposed to be man's best friend, it could be argued that, in the West at least, that honour could equally go to the Horse. For centuries before the motor car and the train, the horse was man's principal means of transport – both for personal journeys and for moving goods from place to place. On the farm, heavy horses pulled the plough so that crops could be sown and months later drew the wagons that carried the harvest to market. Even when the first canals came along, horses were still needed to drag the boats down the waterways.

Without the horse, the economy would have ground to a halt. Even today we still admire horses. We love their grace and beauty and proud demeanour. We recognise that even a tame horse retains a certain wild, unpredictability while true wild horses seem the ultimate free spirits. Despite never actually having ridden a horse, many a desk-bound city-dweller dreams of one day galloping along a deserted beach on horseback.

Instinctively we seem to recognise there's something special about the Horse. In China, too, the Horse is regarded as a symbol of freedom.

So people born in the year of the Horse have a certain magnificence about them. They are cheerful and amicable and tend to have a great many friends. Their physique is strong and athletic with broad shoulders and fine heads of thick hair. Where would the Horse be without its mane? Most Horses excel at sports. They can run fast as you might expect but they will happily try any sport or game until they find the one that suits them best.

Horses, being herd animals are gregarious types and don't like to spend too long alone. They enjoying hanging out with a crowd, chatting and swapping gossip, and Horses of both sexes can lap up any amount of grooming. They love having their hair brushed and fussed over, their nails manicured; a facial or relaxing massage is usually welcome.

Yet Horses are more complex than they first appear. The affable, easy-going charmer delighting everyone at a party, can suddenly take offence at a casual remark or storm off in a huff over some tiny hitch almost unnoticeable to anyone else, leaving companions baffled. They tend to stay baffled too because it's difficult to get a handle on what upsets the Horse since what annoys them one week may leave them completely unruffled the next.

The trouble is, although they look tough, Horses are in fact very sensitive. Inside, they're still half wild. Their senses are incredibly sharp, and although they don't realise it, deep down they're constantly scanning the horizon and sniffing the air for the first signs of danger. As a result, Horses live on their nerves. They tend to over-react when things don't go completely to plan and have to work hard to control a sense of panic. Ideally, Horses would like to bolt away when the going gets rough but as this is not usually possible, they get moody and difficult instead.

Provide calm, congenial conditions for a Horse, however, and you couldn't wish for a friendlier companion. The Horse is lively, enthusiastic, versatile, and fun.

At work, the Horse wants to do well but can't stand being fenced in or forced to perform repetitive, routine tasks. Also, although they're good in a team, Horses have a need for privacy and independence so they may change jobs frequently until they find the right role. Yet when they're happy, Horses will shine.

At home, Horse is probably planning the next trip. Horses like to be comfortable but they're not the most domesticated of the signs. They love being in the open air and don't see the point of spending too much time wallowing on a sofa or polishing dusty ornaments. They may well spend more time in the garden than indoors. On holiday, Horse loves to head for wide open spaces – a vast beach, a craggy hillside or a mountain meadow, Horse would be thrilled to explore them all.

Best Jobs for Horse

Travelling Salesman

Sportsman

Jockey

Hairdresser

Estate Agent

Dog Groomer

Driving Instructor

Party Planner

Perfect Partners

Cupid's arrow can strike anywhere at any time, of course, but once the novelty of new romance wears off, some relationships are easier to maintain than others. Here's a guide to the Horse's compatibility with other signs.

Horse with Horse

No doubt about it, these two make a magnificent couple, and any foals in the family would be spectacular. They certainly understand each other, particularly their shared need for both company and alone time so, in general, they get on well. The only tricky part could come if they both grew anxious over the same issue at the same time. Neither would find it easy to calm the other.

Horse with Goat

Goat and Horse just click! These two love kicking up their heels and trotting off into the green. Goat doesn't need to go far or do anything strenuous but is always up for a break in routine, while Horse doesn't do routine at all so is constantly on the lookout for a partner ready to escape. This couple rarely considers the consequences but, mostly, they don't need to.

Horse with Monkey

Uh oh – best not attempted unless it's love at first sight. Monkey and Horse have wildly different outlooks and can't seem to see eye to eye on anything. They're both lively but in different ways that don't complement each other. Monkey will consider Horse's moods illogical and pointless while Horse is irritated that Monkey makes no attempt to understand how Horse feels. Very hard work.

Horse with Rooster

The eye-catching Rooster intrigues Horse while Rooster appreciates Horse's strength and agility. They can enjoy many stimulating dates together. Yet, in the long-run, this couple may not be able to provide the stability the other needs. They're both sensitive types but in different ways. After a while, the relationship could run out of steam.

Horse with Dog

Both good friends of man, these two can make a formidable team. Dog understands the occasional need for solitude while admiring Horse's strength and agility. Horse, meanwhile, senses Dog's loyalty and down to earth nature. Both lovers of the great outdoors and physical activity, they'll never be short of adventures to share. A promising long-term relationship.

Horse with Pig

Pig and Horse are good companions. Horse is soothed by easy-going Pig and Pig is proud to be seen with such an alluring creature as Horse. They don't have a lot of interests in common but they don't antagonise each other either. They can jog along amicably for quite a while but long-term they may find they each want more than the other can provide.

Horse with Rat

Rat and Horse both fizz with energy and they love action and looking good, yet this is not seen as an ideal partnership. Nothing's impossible of course but these two will have to work hard to find harmony. The Rat will admire Horse's enthusiasm and cheerful approach but become impatient to discover Horse can also be fiery and emotional. Horse, on the other hand, can find Rat's risk-taking behaviour extremely worrying.

Horse with Ox

Long ago on many Western farms, Ox was replaced by the Horse, and it may be that Ox has never forgotten and never forgiven. At any rate, these two, despite both being big, strong animals are not usually friends. Horse is too flighty and frivolous to interest Ox for long, while Ox's methodical, careful ways will irritate the Horse. Best not to go there.

Horse with Tiger

This athletic pair gets on pretty well. They both like physical pursuits, testing their strength out of doors or just enjoying the feel of the wind in their hair and the ground under their feet. True, Horse may not quite understand Tiger's plans for world domination but it doesn't really matter. Horse is happy to be loyal to such a charismatic partner. As they're both moody, there could be rows but making up is exciting.

Horse with Rabbit

This could be tricky. It's fairly unlikely that Horse and Rabbit would ever end up on a date but if they did and there was a strong attraction, it could lead to a love/hate relationship. Rabbit's neat and tidy ways would enrage Horse and Horse's unpredictable moods and over-the-top reactions would annoy Rabbit. Soon, Horse is likely to bolt for the hills or Rabbit retreat to its burrow.

Horse with Dragon

The athletic Horse is pretty good at keeping up with dashing Dragon. And Dragon appreciates a partner who enjoys getting out and about as much as Dragon does. Yet Horse might grow weary of Dragon's constant new projects and resent having to be involved. Horse likes to go off and do Horsey things at frequent intervals which Dragon tends to view as disloyal. This relationship could get fiery.

Horse with Snake

At some level, perhaps Horse remembers how Snake beat him in the calendar race, so despite an initial attraction, these two could be wary of each other. Snake is impressed by Horse's energy and athleticism while Horse admires Snake's elegance and charm. Yet they don't really have much in common. Deep thinking Snake could find Horse rather shallow and Horse may see Snake as frustratingly enigmatic.

Success For the Horse in The Year of the Pig

The glorious zodiac Horse can look forward to an unusual and surprisingly contented year in 2019.

The Horse belongs to the Fire family of signs while the Pig is a Water creature and usually fire and water don't mix too well. Yet the Horse and the Pig – perhaps because they're both domesticated, farmyard animals – tend to be amicable and tolerant of each other. They may not share the same interests, but they don't often fall out.

Since this year belongs to the Earth element, and Fire nurtures Earth in the Chinese cycle, Horses are likely to feel comfortable with the atmosphere and find that events go their way without too much effort and struggle on their part.

Yet despite this, typical Horses may sense that, this year, things are a little different. The Horse is a very active, independent sign with an urge to roam far and wide. In 2019, however, Horse is likely to be quite happy to remain closer to home. In fact, Horses could find themselves enjoying actually being at home much more than usual this year. The familiar Horse restlessness drains away or, at least, is significantly dialled down and Horse friends and family find they are seeing much more of their favourite equine these days.

Horses who are not usually too fussed about the state of their stables could even discover an unexpected interest in home décor and design. For the first time, they begin to understand the fascination often lavished on this area of life by other signs. Many Horses will be remodelling or renovating their homes in 2019 or even planning a house move. This change of behaviour is down to the Earth influence that's prevailed last year and this.

Typical Horses will have done very well in 2018's Year of the Dog because Horses and Dogs are good friends. But the strong Earth energy ushered in by the Dog last year will have excited the Horse into galloping around seizing every opportunity offered, and aiming to complete them all in record time.

The result is that, this year, Horse starts the proceedings feeling a little fatigued, despite the legendary Horse energy and stamina. Yet, since the Pig's Earth energy is of a gentler, more domestic variety, the Horse is finally inspired to ease up a bit and enjoy the rewards from all that past effort. Those sensitive Horse nostrils have also picked up the end of cycle vibe in the air and Horse intuitively understands that now is the perfect time to go with the flow and slow down for a while.

Ironically, just as the Horse is winding down, the rewards for all that hard work from last year begin to show themselves. Horses can expect pay raises, promotions, and significant gains. Careers blossom. Suddenly, the Horse is appreciated, possibly as never before. Or perhaps it's just that the Horse doesn't usually hang around long enough to notice the effect they have on other signs. Whatever the reason, suddenly Horse is surrounded by helpful colleagues and friends, and the affectionate attention only reinforces Horse's out-of-character urge to stay put and bask.

Holidays and plenty of days out in the fresh air are still on the equine calendar, but Horses could find themselves developing an interest in exploring those previously unvisited nooks and crannies closer to home.

Love

Glamorous female Horses can look forward to even more attention than usual. You're never short of besotted admirers, but this year your phone never stops ringing. There are more parties and events than ever, and you're on every guest list. It will be very difficult to make a choice and possibly you won't want to. But Horses who are hoping to settle down could find the perfect partner this year.

Already-settled Horses could find their relationship becoming more blissful this year, probably due to a renewed interest in home building. You know you should have been spending more time with your partner and, this year, Horses are likely to actually put this advice into operation. The beneficial results will amaze you. You could even end up with a little Piglet in the family.

Keys to Success

This year, the Horse can enjoy a good time without even trying. You simply need to manage the rewards from past efforts with care. Resist the temptation to be extravagant or indulge in risky ventures with the extra cash that comes your way. Horses can be inclined to moodiness so don't allow a reckless whim to undo all your previous good work. Unusually for such a well-groomed sign, there's a danger in overindulging in food this year. Enjoy those meals by all means but keep an eye on the scales.

The Horse Year at a Glance

January – Change is in the air. You feel pleasantly stretched from previous efforts and ready for a new direction and new attitude.

February – Something you began last year which was not looking encouraging, unexpectedly begins to bear fruit. You're surprised but pleased.

March – You're ready to relax. Tired but happy, you realise how hard you've been working for such a long time.

April – You're not normally the gambling type, but this month you could be inspired to take a risk. Be very, very careful.

May – Pig likes to eat, drink, and be merry and suddenly so do you Horse. Don't stuff yourself too much.

June – You're flavour of the month with almost everyone, Horse. Whatever you've been doing, do it some more!

July – Finances are looking good. A pay rise or windfall of some kind is on the way. Don't let good fortune go to your head though – pride comes before a fall as they say.

August – Carefree Pig is tempting you to splurge some of that extra cash. Resist unnecessary purchases. Why not open a savings account?

September – Romance is in the air. A fabulous holiday could lead to love.

October – An unwise move you made a little while ago could have repercussions this month. Stay alert. Attend to any issues immediately.

November – A highly sociable month with Horse invited to all the parties. Enjoy.

December – Celebrations are happening all around. Yet, you've been inspired with a brilliant idea. Start planning for next year.

Lucky Colours for 2019: Terracotta, silver, white, purple

Lucky Numbers for 2019: 3, 4, 9

CHAPTER 9: THE GOAT

Goat Years

17 February 1931 – 5 February 1932

5 February 1943 – 24 January 1944

24 January 1955 – 11 February 1956

9 February 1967 – 29 January 1968

28 January 1979 – 15 February 1980

15 February 1991 – 3 February 1992

1 February 2003 – 21 January 2004

19 February 2015 – 7 February 2016

6 February 2027 – 25 January 2028

Natural Element: Fire

Sometimes known as the sign of the Sheep, though more often the Goat, this delightful sign is one of the happiest in the zodiac. The confusion over the name is thought to have occurred over differing translations of a Chinese symbol which could mean either Goat or Sheep. These days, the interpretation 'Goat' seems to be more widely used. But what's in a name? Either way, in China this sign is regarded as the symbol of peace.

Flesh and blood goats, of course, can be pretty lively at times; a male billy-goat with its sharp horns can be downright aggressive and difficult. What's more, goats can be surprisingly stubborn. Yet the zodiac Goat has left most of these qualities behind and emerges as a sweet, gentle, imaginative creature.

People born in a Goat year tend to be the nicest characters. They are tolerant and friendly, have no wish to be competitive, and want to see the best in everyone they meet. Though they may not realise it, this attitude often unconsciously brings out the best in others so the Goat's expectations are usually fulfilled. The Goat has a quiet knack of getting on with almost everyone, even people that others can't abide. In fact, Goats can find it quite upsetting the way some people seem to be so unjustly disliked.

The Goat is the true artist of the zodiac. Wonderfully creative with a fine eye for colour and design, the Goat loves beautiful things and even sees beauty in objects and places that hold no appeal for others. Most Goats have some natural artistic talent so whether it's painting, sculpting, writing poetry, knitting, or some creative skill they've invented themselves, the Goat will happily spend hours working on their art.

Concepts such as time and also money, have little meaning for the Goat. When the Goat gets lost in inspiration, hours pass in seconds and Goat ends up late for anything else that might have been on the timetable. Goat is continually baffled by this strange phenomenon.

Similarly, money is frustrating for the Goat. Goats are not materialistic, neither are they particularly ambitious in a worldly way. Objects other people regard as status symbols hold little Goat appeal so they can't see the point of putting in a lot of energy to acquire them. For this reason, Goats are not career-driven. All they really want to do is pursue their artistic project but if this won't provide an income, they'll do their best at whatever job turns up, in order to get back to their true interests at weekends.

The perfect scenario for the Goat would be a big win on the lottery so that they never have to waste time on a conventional job again. Unfortunately, though, because Goats are not good at handling finances, they'd probably have to get someone else to look after the cash otherwise it could evaporate with distressing speed.

Goats are notoriously impractical with matters such as bills, household repairs, filling in forms, and meeting deadlines. They just can't seem to get round to such mundane items. Though they're intelligent people, they'll frequently claim not to understand such things. The truth is, of course, the ultra-creative Goat brain just can't be bothered. And no matter how many times Goats get into trouble for this carelessness, they don't learn from their mistakes.

What's more, though they hate arguments and don't bear grudges, Goats can suddenly dig their heels in over what looks to others like a trivial matter and stick stubbornly to a decision no matter how poor the outcome is likely to be.

The Goat home is an intriguing place. Striking and original, it's likely to be filled with mismatched treasures Goat has picked up along the way. Goats love car boot sales, junk shops, and galleries. They enjoy beach-combing and collecting branches and broken wood on country walks. They've even been known to 'rescue' items from rubbish skips. Somehow Goat manages to weave together the most unpromising items to create a pleasing effect.

On holiday, Goat likes to carry on in the same way as at weekends – pottering around in interesting places seeking out treasures and discovering new talent. Warm, sunny places are beneficial for the Goat constitution so visits to countries such as Italy and Greece, renowned for their art, would be ideal.

Best Jobs for Goat

Painter

Ceramic Workshop Worker

Musician

Beautician

Charity Worker

Garden Designer

Colour Therapist

Antiques Restorer

Potter

Perfect Partners

Cupid's arrow can strike anywhere at any time, of course, but once the novelty of new romance wears off, some relationships are easier to maintain than others. Here's a guide to the Goat's compatibility with other signs.

Goat with Goat

When things are going well, you won't find a happier couple than two Goats. They are perfectly in tune with each other's creative natures and understand when to do things together and when to step back and give the other space. And since they both share the same interests, their together times are always fun. Yet, when practical problems arise, neither can easily cope. With a helpful friend on speed-dial, this would work.

Goat with Monkey

Monkey and Goat are different but in a good way. Though they don't quite 'get' each other deep down, Goat admires Monkey's lively personality and magical ability to come up with solutions for everything, while curious Monkey enjoys Goat's knowledge of the arts and the unusual. Long-term, Goat might not present enough of a challenge for Monkey but, with effort, it's a promising match.

Goat with Rooster

Peaceful Goat is not one to make feathers fly so these two are unlikely to fall out, but they're unlikely to find perfect compatibility either. Goat is unable to give Rooster the regular ego boosts that make Rooster thrive while Rooster is baffled by Goat's unpredictable devotion to impractical projects or people. Misunderstandings are likely.

Goat with Dog

This is another relationship that could be tricky. Loyal Dog would be quite willing to stand by Goat when practical problems loom but could end up irritated by Goat's inability to learn from previous mistakes and so keeps making them. Goat can't understand why Dog gets so bothered. With care, these two could learn to live together.

Goat with Pig

Happy-go-lucky Pig and laid-back Goat make a good pair. They hate to stir up trouble and always look for a peaceful solution to any challenge. Ideally, they'd avoid the challenge altogether. They could be very contented together as long as Pig's spending and Goat's inability to deal with finances doesn't get them into trouble.

Goat with Rat

The Rat is charmed by carefree Goat and fascinated by its artistic talent and happy knack of living in the present. Easy-going Goat tends to like everyone so is perfectly content to enjoy Rat's company. These two can get along fine, yet they don't really understand each other deep down. Long-term, the Rat may find Goat's lack of interest in the practical side of life irritating.

Goat with Ox

Though these two share artistic natures (even if in the case of the Ox, they're well hidden), deep down they don't 'get' one another. Ox may be beguiled at first by Goat's friendly, easy-going manner but then disappointed to discover Goat seems to find everyone equally delightful, even those who are plainly unworthy. Goat, on the other hand, can't understand why Ox won't lighten up more. This relationship would require a lot of effort and compromise.

Goat with Tiger

Tiger and Goat don't have a lot in common. While their aims and temperaments are quite different, they are both sociable creatures and Goat wouldn't mind Tiger attracting all the attention when they're out together. Tiger in return would appreciate Goat's lack of jealousy and generosity of spirit. Yet, long-term, they're likely to drift apart as they follow their different interests.

Goat with Dragon

Goat tends to baffle the busy Dragon. Dragon can see Goat is the creative type but can't understand why Goat doesn't appear to be working very hard when so much could be achieved. In fact, if they stayed together long enough, Dragon could help Goat make the most of many talents but it's unlikely either of them can sustain enough interest for this to happen.

Goat with Snake

Snake and Goat could enjoy many happy hours touring art galleries and exhibitions together. Neither of them craves excitement and harsh, adrenalin-boosting activities and both appreciate creative, artistic personalities. There's no pressure to compete with each other so these two would sail along quite contentedly. Not a passionate alliance but they could be happy.

Goat with Horse

Goat and Horse just click! These two love kicking up their heels and trotting off into the green. Goat doesn't need to go far or do anything strenuous but is always up for a break in routine, while Horse doesn't do routine at all so is constantly on the lookout for a partner ready to escape. This couple rarely considers the consequences, but mostly, they don't need to.

Success For the Goat in The Year of the Pig

Sure-footed Goats of the zodiac have got an enjoyable year to look forward to in 2019. The Year of the Pig is good news for Goats everywhere. This is because the Pig and the Goat are usually firm friends. They manage this despite the fact that the Goat belongs to the Fire family of creatures while the Pig is regarded as a Water sign and, normally, fire and water don't work well together.

Perhaps their secret is that though both are originally wild animals, Goats and Pigs are now usually found in the farmyard; both are a similar size and, at least as far as their celestial symbols are concerned, both are gentle, easy-going personalities. Neither the Goat nor the Pig is bothered about trying to get the upper hand. They're both content to potter along as pleasantly as possible. So, in 2019, the Goat can expect to avoid major conflicts and unwelcome outside interference in Goat affairs.

What's more, the Earth element of the year is sympathetic to Fire signs, since Fire is believed to nurture Earth in the Chinese cycle, so this is another bonus for Goats. Last year, while quite a few of the zodiac creatures were having a tough time under the exacting influence of the Earth Dog, most Goats trotted away relatively unscathed. This year is likely to be even easier, as the Earth element is repeated but in its softer, more feminine form which will be even kinder to Goats.

The Goat is a very creative sign, and 2019 is likely to see a big expansion for all Goats involved in artistic, design, or entertainment-oriented businesses – areas which hold a particular appeal for the Pig. Those Goats who manage to restrain their more whacky ideas and combine the original with the familiar will do best of all, though, as the earth element doesn't appreciate too much eccentricity. Goats working in other fields can also expect to do well this year though they're not quite as favoured as their more creative cousins.

The most striking improvements in 2019 are likely to be around blockages or obstacles that stood in the Goat path last year despite the general good fortune.

These blockages could have been financial – many Goats would have found requests for loans rejected or delayed; legal – property purchases ran into unexpected hitches; or personal – someone at work or at home proved obstructive and prevented a number of Goats from achieving all they'd hoped to achieve.

Well, the good news is that under the watery influence of the Pig, these obstacles will be washed away. Suddenly, funds become available, legal issues proceed smoothly, and those irritating people who put boulders in Goat's path will either move on or develop a pleasing change of heart. At last, Goats can go ahead with all those plans and ambitions that had to be put on hold last year.

Goats tend not to be too bothered about finances, but in 2019 their bank managers are likely to be much more pleased with them as increased funds begin to flow into Goat accounts. Yet most Goats, who need little encouragement from shopaholic Pigs at the best of times, will find plenty of delightful ways to spend the extra cash.

At work, the talents of creative Goats will be noticed and appreciated more than usual and rewards will follow. Despite the fact that typical Goats are not particularly interested in climbing to the top of company structures, many could be offered promotion this year.

There is also the chance that the Goat will find unusual new premises in 2019 – either to live in or work from. Self-employed Goats could well stumble across an unlikely building that would make an ideal studio or workshop, for instance, and they use their artistic skill to transform it. Moving into this innovative place will prove lucky.

Other Goats who don't normally have an outlet for their creative gifts will find themselves drawn to evening classes, training courses, or new hobbies that will develop their skills. They could become so successful that one day this new talent could lead to a new career.

Most Goats will be quite happy at home this year, redecorating the house, growing something beautiful in the garden, or practising that new hobby but they'll also get the chance for a number of interesting breaks not too far afield.

Love

Single Goats will be looking particularly stylish this year in their own special, quirky way and this will attract a lot of attention. Yet, even when very much wanting a long-term partner, the single Goat will not settle for a dull, conventional match. Goats have enough interests to amuse themselves and won't get serious with anyone who doesn't properly appreciate their many qualities, even though they're not averse to frequent, very light flirtations. 2019, however, may be the year Mr or Ms Right shows up – probably at some artistic event or entertainment.

Goats already spoken for should have a happy year, but they need to remember to make time for their partner. Too great a devotion to a new creative project or hobby could lead to resentment – unless, of course, the partner is another Goat, in which case they'll be so happily absorbed in their own thing they probably won't notice.

Keys to Success

Goats tend not to be too bothered about the conventional idea of success and, in any case, this year they've got so much going for them they don't need to worry too much. Yet, even bigger improvements and breakthroughs can be made in 2019 if they remain vigilant so they can instantly spot the moment when a barrier that has been holding them up in the past suddenly dissolves. The quicker the Goat leaps in and makes the most of the new opportunity, the further along the path to their goal they'll get. Despite this, Goats should also think very carefully about any creation or scheme that's too far ahead of its time. The earth element rarely supports ventures that are wild and 'off the wall'. If you've reinvented the wheel, only much better, it's probably best to wait till 2020!

The Goat Year at a Glance

January – Already new ideas are brewing, and you're inspired to try something fresh or adopt a novel approach to your usual way of doing things.

February – You're keen to revamp your look and give your wardrobe a makeover. A whole new image seems exciting.

March – Whatever you did last month seems to have heads turning in your direction. New romance is on offer.

April – Jealousy is in the air. Two-timing in relationships will be found out. You may not care.

May – Things are going well at work. Your efforts are noticed and appreciated. For once you get the credit.

June – Work gets better and better. Promotion, a new job, or a pay rise could be discussed. Be prepared.

July – A disruptive person from the past reappears. Don't allow them to muddy the waters.

August – Keep smiling and doing what you know to do. Everything is proceeding well.

September – Romance is getting hotter. You may have to make a decision. Follow your heart.

October – Avoid risks at work, particularly anything finance-related.

November – Someone close has made a mistake. Be ready to be supportive but don't lend money.

December – Family and friends are in the mood to celebrate. You're inspired to do something memorable.

Lucky Colours for 2019: Blue, Red, Yellow
Lucky Numbers for 2019: 6, 14

CHAPTER 10: THE MONKEY

Monkey Years

6 February 1932 – 25 January 1933

25 January 1944 – 12 February 1945

12 February 1956 – 30 January 1957

30 January 1968 – 16 February 1969

16 February 1980 – 4 February 1981

4 February 1992 – 22 January 1993

22 January 2004 – 8 February 2005

8 February 2016 – 27 January 2017

26 January 2028 – 12 February 2029

Natural Element: Metal

Man's closest relative, the clever, playful Monkey is the star of many a wildlife documentary, while the monkey enclosure at any zoo is usually surrounded by fascinated visitors. We're awed by the agility and energy of the monkey and intrigued by its resourcefulness. True, in some countries where monkeys are found in the wild, they can be regarded as a nuisance around human habitations but, in general, we're very fond of the monkey.

So intelligent is this creature it's not surprising that people born under the sign of the Monkey are regarded as near geniuses. In China, the Monkey is connected with justice and wisdom. Perhaps this impression gave rise to the famous folklore characters the 'three wise monkeys' – See no evil, Hear no evil, Speak no evil.

Like their namesakes, people born under the sign of Monkey tend to be physically agile. They're quick-moving, quick-thinking types with glittering wit and charismatic personalities. At a party, the Monkey will be in the centre of the group that's convulsed with laughter. Monkeys love jokes and humour of all kinds, and if anyone's going to start entertaining the crowd with a few magic tricks, it's likely to be a Monkey.

While not necessarily conventionally good-looking, the Monkey's lively face and sparkling eyes are always attractive and Monkeys have no difficulty in acquiring partners. The tricky bit for a Monkey is staying around long enough to build a relationship.

People born under this sign need constant mental stimulation. They don't necessarily expect others to provide it. They are quite happy to amuse themselves with puzzles, conundrums, the mending of broken objects, and inventing things, but they also need new places and new faces. Few signs can keep up with Monkey's constant motion.

What's more, Monkeys are not good with rules or authority. They've seldom seen a rule they don't want to break or avoid. In fact, it sometimes seems as if Monkey deliberately seeks out annoying regulations just for the fun of finding a way around them.

Yet beneath the humour and games, the Monkey is ambitious with an astute brain. Monkeys can turn their hand to almost anything and make a success of it, but they're probably best suited to working for themselves. If anyone is going to benefit from their efforts they believe it should be, chiefly, themselves. Also, they're not good at taking orders and, to be fair, they're so clever they don't need to. They can usually see the best way to carry out a task better than anyone else.

The Monkey home is often a work in progress. Monkey is always looking for a quicker, easier, cheaper, or more efficient way of doing everything and new ideas could encompass the entire building from the plumbing to the lighting and novel security systems. The first home in the street to be operated by remote control is likely to be the Monkey's. Yet, chances are, Monkey would prefer to meet friends in a nearby restaurant.

When it comes to holidays, Monkeys can have a bag packed seemingly in seconds and are ready to be off anywhere, anytime. They don't much mind where they go as long as it's interesting, unusual, and offers plenty to be discovered. Lying on a sun-lounger for extended periods does not appeal.

Best Jobs for Monkey

Inventor

Barrister

Magician

Journalist

Photographer

IT Expert

Perfect Partners

Cupid's arrow can strike anywhere at any time, of course, but once the novelty of new romance wears off, some relationships are easier to maintain than others. Here's a guide to the Monkey compatibility with other signs.

Monkey with Monkey

It's not always the case that opposites attract. More often like attracts like and when two Monkeys get together, they find each other delightful. At last, they've met another brain as quick and agile as their own and a person who relishes practical jokes as much as they do. What's more, this is a partner that shares a constant need for change and novelty. Yet, despite this, two Monkeys can often end up competing with each other. As long as they can recognise this, and laugh about it, they'll be fine.

Monkey with Rooster

While not a perfect match, these two have got a lot of time for each other. Monkey recognises the intelligent brain beneath Rooster's plumage while Rooster admires Monkey's ability to entertain a crowd and they both adore socialising. They could enjoy many fun dates together. Long-term, though, Rooster may tire of Monkey's jokes.

Monkey with Dog

Monkey finds Dog intriguing. Monkey senses Dog's strength of character coupled with its playful streak which fits well with Monkey's love of games. Dog, meanwhile, appreciates Monkey's energy and light-hearted approach. Yet, before long, Monkey's disdain for rules will grate on Dog's instinctive love of them. They cannot agree in this area, and it could lead to arguments.

Monkey with Pig

On the surface, these two might seem an unlikely couple. Yet Pig enjoys Monkey's fun and humour while Monkey is happy to be admired uncritically. What's more, Monkey's inventive mind can solve any difficulties caused by Pig's spending and since Monkey can't resist a challenge, the opportunity to retrain Pig, or at least find a way to obtain purchases cheaper, could help the relationship last.

Monkey with Rat

Unlikely as it might appear, mischievous Monkey and the clever Rat make a good partnership. Their quick minds, sociable natures, and love of novelty ensure that they're never bored together. True, Rat might sometimes feel that Monkey is too inclined to skim over the surface of things and could do with being more serious at times but Monkey's ingenuity and audaciousness always saves the day. Both can have a weakness for gambling though, so need to take care.

Monkey with Ox

The naughty Monkey scandalises Ox but in such an amusing way that Ox can't help laughing. Monkey, on the other hand, is equally amused to find an audience so easy to shock. This unlikely pair enjoy each other's company and get on surprisingly well. Yet, right from the start, it's probably obvious to both that a long-term relationship couldn't last. A fun flirtation, though, could be a terrific tonic for them both.

Monkey with Tiger

Tiger can't help being intrigued by sparkling Monkey and Monkey is flattered by such interest. Who wouldn't enjoy being admired by such a fabulous creature? But irrepressible Monkey just can't help teasing, and being teased is not a sensation Tiger is familiar with (or appreciates). Unless the attraction is very strong, these two will wind each other up until they can bear it no longer and part.

Monkey with Rabbit

Mercurial Monkey doesn't really 'get' Rabbit. The Monkey can appreciate how well Rabbit operates and sees this approach gets good results, but it's all too picky and slow for Monkey. Rabbit, on the other hand, is amused by Monkey's quick wit and clever ways but deplores Monkey's slapdash, sometimes devious tactics. Very unlikely to work out.

Monkey with Dragon

These two are likely to hit it off immediately. Each is attracted to the other's intelligence and lively presence, and Dragon's exuberance doesn't overwhelm hyperactive Monkey. What's more, although they both enjoy being surrounded by a crowd, Monkey only wants to make people laugh while Dragon hopes to inspire them to a cause. There is no conflict, so this couple can help each other to go far.

Monkey with Snake

These two clever creatures ought to admire each other, if only for their fine minds and, at first, it's possible they might. But unless they're really determined to make it work, it won't be long before active Monkey finds Snake's energy-saving ways irritating, while Snake loses patience with Monkey's endless jokes.

Monkey with Horse

Uh oh – best not attempted unless it's love at first sight. Monkey and Horse have wildly different outlooks and can't seem to see eye to eye on anything. They're both lively but in different ways that don't complement each other. Monkey will consider Horse's moods illogical and pointless while Horse is irritated that Monkey makes no attempt to understand how Horse feels. Very hard work.

Monkey with Goat

Monkey and Goat are different but in a good way. Though they don't quite 'get' each other deep down, Goat admires Monkey's lively personality and magical ability to come up with solutions for everything, while curious Monkey enjoys Goat's knowledge of the arts and the unusual. Long-term, Goat might not present enough of a challenge for Monkey but, with effort, it's a promising match.

Success For the Monkey in The Year of the Pig

The clever Monkey looks set to have an intriguing year in 2019 – which is just the way the ever-curious Monkey likes it. The Monkey and the Pig get on well even though the Monkey lives in the wild and in surroundings far more exotic than most Pigs will ever encounter, while the Pig is a real stay-at-home as far as Monkey is concerned. Each is content to enjoy the others' foibles without trying to change them too much.

What's more, the Monkey belongs to the Metal family of creatures while the Pig is regarded as a water animal. The metal element is believed to be nurturing of water in the Chinese cycle so the Pig feels comfortable with Monkey around – though sometimes Monkey can get fatigued if Pig is too demanding.

Then again, last year's Earth element is repeated in 2019 but in a gentler, softer form, and Earth is believed to nurture Metal in the Chinese cycle. So the Monkey can expect to feel supported in the Year of the Pig but is also likely to be required to give support at times.

This friendly but contradictory pulling and pushing are what's likely to give 2019 its intriguing quality and a certain edge that was missing from last year. The Monkey will need to remain alert and ready to spring in either direction when the occasion demands – probably out of the blue. Yet, versatile Monkeys are not only perfectly capable of doing this, they positively relish the challenge. The worst situation for a Monkey is unchanging dullness.

Last year should have been good for the Monkey career, for those primates typical of their sign. This year, all that continues, but events are beginning to flow faster. More opportunities are pouring in and, with them, more responsibilities. It's very tempting for the Monkey to say 'yes' to everything but this could be a mistake. The demanding Pig could drain even energetic Monkey's enviable energy, and a tired Monkey could make expensive mistakes. Monkeys involved in catering or any business concerning food or food production will be especially fortunate.

Unusually, it seems as if many Monkeys could find themselves working more than one job this year. This appeals to the Monkey's versatile mind. Most Monkeys have so many talents; it's difficult for them to decide which one to pursue. In 2019, it seems they don't have to choose just one. They will get the chance to run several careers or interests side by side.

Perhaps this is the reason why it looks as if the Monkey will enjoy several different streams of income in the Year of the Pig. Cash is rolling in this year in a very pleasing way, Monkey. As with all the signs, encouraged by the extravagant Pig, Monkeys will encounter more ways of spending money than of earning it, and they're likely to be tempted by plenty of shiny, novel items that are hard to resist. Nevertheless, the Monkey that manages to avoid wasteful purchases could use the cash to invest in one of their brilliant, inventive new ideas instead. This could be the perfect moment to launch into something big Monkey – as long as it's not too completely ground-breaking. The Earth element favours twists on the familiar and the homely, rather than the completely different and unseen.

Monkeys can also expect to be in demand this year to give help and support. This may occur at work where experienced Monkeys may be asked to mentor newcomers or assist in teaching technology to less-skilled workmates. Or it may be at home. Perhaps friends or neighbours will be in need of solutions from the lightning Monkey brain. No matter which direction they come from, accept as many of these appeals as possible, Monkey, and luck will follow. Good deeds and kindness attract favour in Earth years.

Love

Both single and attached Monkeys love to flirt and play the field which can cause problems with partners prone to jealousy. The Monkey means no harm but likes variety in all things, and potential lovers need to be able to accept this. In 2019, the Monkey – particularly the female Monkey – is going to be pretty irresistible to all the signs of the zodiac. This is ideal from the Monkey's point of view, but it could cause a long-running relationship to come to an abrupt end. Since Monkey is unlikely to be broken-hearted, this is probably a good thing.

Firmly attached Monkeys will enjoy a sociable year with their partner. They'll be going out and about more than usual and, having come this far, their partner will understand that just because Monkey disappears at a party and spends most of the evening chatting to someone else, there is no threat to their relationship. Knowing each other so well, and having developed their own ways of dealing with Monkey's restlessness, they'll each have a fabulous time and then savour comparing notes when they get home.

Keys to Success

There is little to hold the Monkey back in 2019. Everything should go Monkey's way. Problems are only likely to occur if the Monkey attempts to take on too much and becomes exhausted. It takes quite a lot to fatigue the Monkey – a naturally hyperactive sign – but this year there is such a lot going on, it could happen. What's more, since this is such an unusual state of affairs for the Monkey, they may not know how to deal with it if it happens. Wise Monkeys will pace themselves carefully and timetable plenty of rest and relaxation.

The Monkey Year at a Glance

January – Family members may be in awkward mood this month. Be sympathetic but keep out of their affairs. Concentrate on career.

February – You may spy another opportunity or an additional source of income. Don't rush in but check it out carefully.

March – Jealousy around a relationship seems to grow. Is it imagination or does something need attending to?

April – The boss is looking at you with favour. A pay rise may be forthcoming. Finances are looking up.

May – Good fortune or a win of some kind looks possible. This is unearned income. Don't take risks but a flutter on the lottery may pay off.

June – Now's the time to take a break. Use some of that extra cash for a holiday or take up a new sport or exercise class.

July – Study or training to further your career will bring good fortune. Check out what's on offer.

August – A lucky month. Love is in the air – possibly a holiday romance, or a new face from overseas arrives.

September – Those family disputes could arise again. Try to stay on the fringes but help out if asked.

October – Things are settling down, and you can concentrate on work. A new opportunity is offered with increased rewards.

November – If you were thinking of changing your job, this would be the ideal month. Watch out for jealousy in love.

December – You're in the mood to party. Finally, those tricky relatives are ready to join the fun. A happy time for all.

Lucky Colours for 2019: Yellow, Gold, Pink, White

Lucky Numbers for 2019: 1, 7, 8

CHAPTER 11: THE ROOSTER

Rooster Years

26 January 1933 – 13 February 1934

13 February 1945 – 1 February 1946

31 January 1957 – 17 February 1958

17 February 1969 – 5 February 1970

5 February 1981 – 24 January 1982

23 January 1993 – 9 February 1994

9 February 2005 – 28 January 2006

28 January 2017 – 15 February 2018

13 February 2029 – 2 February 2030

Natural Element: Metal

Colourful, bold, and distinctly noisy, the Rooster rules the farmyard. Seemingly fearless and relishing the limelight, this bird may be small but he doesn't appear to know it. We're looking at a giant personality here. This creature may be the bane of late sleepers, and only a fraction of the size of other animals on the farm, but the Rooster doesn't care. Rooster struts around, puffing out his tiny chest as if he owns the place.

The Chinese associate the Rooster with courage and it's easy to see why. You'd have to be brave to square up to all comers armed only with a modest beak, a couple of sharp claws, and a piercing shriek. Yet Rooster is quite prepared to take on the challenge.

People born in the year of the Rooster tend to be gorgeous to look at and like to dress flamboyantly. Even if their physique is not as slender as it could be, the Rooster is not going to hide it away in drab, black outfits. Roosters enjoy colour and style and they dress to be noticed. These are not shy retiring types. They like attention and they do whatever they can to get it.

Roosters are charming and popular with quick minds and engaging repartee. They have to guard against a tendency to boast but this happens mainly when they sense a companion's interest is wandering. And since they're natural raconteurs, they can usually recapture attention and pass their stories off as good entertainment.

Like the feathered variety, Roosters can be impetuous and impulsive. They tend to rush into situations and commitments that are far too demanding, without a second thought and then later, wonder frantically how they're going to manage. Oddly enough, they usually make things work but only after ferocious effort. Roosters just can't help taking a risk.

Although they're gregarious and often surrounded by friends, there's a sense that deep down, few people know the real Rooster. Underneath the bright plumage and cheerful banter, Rooster is quite private and a little vulnerable. Perhaps Roosters fear they'll disappear or get trampled on if they don't make enough noise. So they need frequent reassurance that they're liked and appreciated.

With all the emphasis Rooster puts on the splendid Rooster appearance it's often overlooked that, in fact, the Rooster has a good brain and is quite a thinker. Roosters keep up with current affairs, they're shrewd with money and business matters, and though you never see them doing it, in private they're busily reading up on all the latest information on their particular field.

At work, Rooster wants to be the boss and often ends up that way. Failing that, Roosters will go it alone and start their own business. They're usually successful due to the Rooster's phenomenal hard work but when things do go wrong it's likely to be down to the Rooster's compulsion to take a risk or promise more than it's possible to deliver. Also, while being sensitive to criticism themselves, Roosters can be extremely frank in putting across their views to others. They may pride themselves on their plain-speaking but it may not do them any favours with customers and employees.

Rooster thinks the home should be a reflection of its owner's splendid image so, if at all possible, it will be lavish, smart, and full of enviable items. They have good taste, in a colourful way, and don't mind spending money on impressive pieces. If the Rooster can be persuaded to take a holiday, a five-star hotel in a prestigious location with plenty of socialising would be ideal, or a luxury cruise with a place at the Captain's table.

Best Jobs for Rooster

Managing Director

Fashion Buyer

Mayor

MP

The Military (Officer Level)

Hairdresser

Make-up artist

Theatre Director

Perfect Partners

Cupid's arrow can strike anywhere at any time, of course, but once the novelty of new romance wears off, some relationships are easier to maintain than others. Here's a guide to the Rooster's compatibility with other signs.

Rooster with Rooster

Fabulous to look at though they would be, these two alpha creatures would find it difficult to share the limelight. They can't help admiring each other at first sight but since both needs to be the boss, there could be endless squabbles for dominance. What's more, neither would be able to give the other the regular reassurance they need. Probably not worth attempting.

Rooster with Dog

Rooster and Dog are not the best of partners. Dog can be as plain-spoken as Rooster and is not likely to be impressed by overt show. What's more, Dog is often critical and Rooster can't stand criticism. Rooster, on the other hand, is likely to sense and resent Dog's attitude. Frustration abounds for both in this relationship. Only for the hopelessly love-struck.

Rooster with Pig

These two might seem an unlikely couple – modest Pig with extrovert Rooster. Yet Pig has no need or wish to crow and can see the vulnerable character that lurks beneath Rooster's fine feathers; Rooster, meanwhile, responds to Pig's kindness and undemanding nature. As long as Rooster doesn't get bored, this can be a contented relationship.

Rooster with Rat

The first thing Rat notices about the Rooster is its beautiful plumage, but this is a relationship which is unlikely to get much further than initial admiration. Rooster's direct and frank approach can strike the Rat as tactless, while the Rooster can't understand why Rat has to make life so convoluted and complicated. Then again, Rooster's natural confidence and aplomb can come across as bragging to the Rat. These two have to be very determined to make a partnership work.

Rooster with Ox

For all its bravado and showing off, the Rooster is a down-to-earth type, drawn to security and accumulating the good things in life – requirements that Ox understands very well and can supply effortlessly. What's more, Ox can't help but admire Rooster's fine feathers and skill at communicating in a crowd – attributes Ox doesn't have and is unlikely to acquire. These two could enjoy a very good partnership.

Rooster with Tiger

The only feathered creature in the zodiac, the opulence and novelty of Rooster's appearance will draw Tiger like a magnet. What's more, deep down they are both quite serious-minded types so on one level they'll have much to share. Yet, despite this, they're not really on the same wavelength and misunderstandings will keep recurring. Could be hard work.

Rooster with Rabbit

A difficult match. However unfair it seems, Rooster comes over as loud, boastful, and uncouth to Rabbit while Rabbit appears dull, staid, and insufficiently admiring of Rooster's fine feathers to appeal to Rooster. These two just can't see below the surface of the other and it would be surprising if they ended up together. Only to be considered by the very determined.

Rooster with Dragon

A Dragon and Rooster pairing will always attract attention. These two are both gorgeous beings and love to be surrounded by admirers. They will probably enjoy going out together and being seen as a couple, but in the long-term they may not be able to provide the kind of support each secretly needs. Entertaining for a while but probably not a lasting relationship.

Rooster with Snake

Surprisingly, Snake and Rooster work well together. Both gorgeous in different ways, they complement each other without competing. Snake's keen eyes can see beneath Rooster's proud facade to the sensitive, unsure person inside, while Rooster appreciates Snake's unobtrusive strength and wise words of encouragement at just the right moment. These two could be inseparable.

Rooster with Horse

The eye-catching Rooster intrigues Horse while Rooster appreciates Horse's strength and agility. They can enjoy many stimulating dates together. Yet, in the long-run, this couple may not be able to provide the stability the other needs. They're both sensitive types but in different ways. After a while, the relationship could run out of steam.

Rooster with Goat

Peaceful Goat is not one to make feathers fly, so these two are unlikely to fall out, but they're unlikely to find perfect compatibility either. Goat is unable to give Rooster the regular ego boosts that make Rooster thrive while Rooster is baffled by Goat's unpredictable devotion to impractical projects or people. Misunderstandings are likely.

Rooster with Monkey

While not a perfect match, these two have got a lot of time for each other. Monkey recognises the intelligent brain beneath Rooster's plumage while Rooster admires Monkey's ability to entertain a crowd and they both adore socialising. They could enjoy many fun dates together. Long-term, though, Rooster may tire of Monkey's jokes.

Success For the Rooster in The Year of the Pig

This is the year proud Roosters can finally spread their wings and fly. Where last year there were frustrations that prevented the typical Rooster from soaring as it should, 2019 is likely to be the year that sets Rooster free. Or at least as free as the Rooster wishes to be.

The Year of the Pig is a welcome break for Roosters. These two farmyard companions may appear to be as different as it's possible for two creatures to be, but although they don't completely understand each other, they share their space quite amicably.

Like the Monkey, the Rooster belongs to the Metal family of zodiac animals while the Pig is regarded as a Water creature. This is helpful because, in the Chinese cycle, Metal nurtures Water so the Pig likes having Rooster around and Rooster feels appreciated in the Pig's company.

What's more, 2019 is an Earth element year and Earth nurtures Metal in the Chinese cycle, so Roosters also benefit from an atmosphere that's generally supportive for 12 months.

Last year was also an Earth element year so typical Roosters should have seen some positive progress; but 2018 was also ruled by the Dog and, unfortunately, the Dog and the Rooster don't get on too well. Chances are, there were plenty of beneficial changes along the way, but they arrived in an abrupt and challenging manner. Many Roosters could have found this frustrating. Roosters like to feel in control, and though the changes were basically welcome, they tended to occur at a time of Dog's choosing not the Rooster's. This would have dented the Rooster's essential but fragile self-confidence.

Well, the good news for Roosters is that 2019 is going to be different. The pressure is off. Happy Pig just wants Rooster to have a good time. The changes made last year will stay in place but now Rooster has a chance to build on them and develop them into a shape and direction that suits the Rooster best. The Rooster is back in charge and, as a result, Rooster's confidence grows. Soon Roosters everywhere will get the chance to open those colourful wings and fly.

Roosters have excellent managerial skills and many individuals born under this sign will find themselves called upon to exercise them in 2019. Some will be promoted into a management role, others already in such a role could end up with more staff and greater responsibilities. Naturally, increased cash will follow, and the Rooster may well be inspired to spend some of it on a long-distance holiday.

Most signs this year will prefer to stay closer to home under the domestic influence of the Earth element, but the Rooster is likely to be the exception. With confidence restored, Roosters could be eager to display their magnificence far and wide.

This is probably not the ideal year for Roosters to launch a new business; it's more a time for consolidating previous gains. Yet since Roosters feel so much better, they're tempted to strike out on their own. Perhaps 2019 is better spent researching and planning and checking the details – particularly as the impulsive Pig is notoriously careless with picky fine print. When you think you've considered every angle, Rooster, leave it a fortnight or better still a month, and look at it again.

Many Roosters will have moved home last year, possibly in something of a rush, so this year they will find they finally have the time and some spare cash to start getting the place how they want it. Contented Rooster weekends are likely to be spent parading around the stores choosing impressive items to display to all their friends.

The only drawback Rooster must be alert to, is a tendency to rush around trying to do too much and make up for lost time. Since Metal nurtures Water, Roosters will find themselves called upon to help out with many Pig-inspired schemes and situations. This is very satisfying, but Roosters are not as tough as they look. The wise Rooster will select – with care – the best places to put their efforts and take all opportunities to relax.

Love

A delightful year for romance looks likely for single Roosters. With confidence back, and plumage gleaming, the single Rooster is a sight to behold, and admirers will crowd around. Enormously enjoyable to the Rooster ego, of course, but something more unusual could be about to occur. As the Rooster basks in the attention, their eyes are likely to meet another pair of eyes across the room, and it's love at first sight. Even Roosters who don't believe in love at first sight are likely to be smitten. Roosters can make devoted partners and this new love could last and last.

Roosters in long-term relationships should find they're more in tune with their partners this year. Past passion can be rediscovered after the upheavals of last year, and the pair may decide to go off and travel the world together.

Keys to Success

Success comes much more easily to the Rooster this year. Yet, in itself, this success could hold an element of danger. Roosters are prone to boastfulness when things are going well and in 2019, with the Rooster confidence restored, there's a chance that admiration will go to Rooster's head. Naturally, friends and colleagues find this irritating at best. Rivals could become downright hostile. This year, the Rooster will flourish if it works hard on remaining modest and magnanimous at all times. Accept compliments gracefully and lavish praise on others.

The Rooster Year at a Glance

January – Good times are coming. You're feeling stronger and more optimistic already.

February – Someone at work is looking at you with approval. The boss is taking an interest. Stay calm and efficient to make the most.

March – A quarrelsome colleague or neighbour could try to make trouble. Watch that fiery temper Rooster. They won't succeed if you ignore the provocation.

April – A brilliant idea occurs. Your entrepreneurial brain instantly springs into action. Check it out but don't rush in just yet.

May – You're flavour of the month at work and socially. A new job, a promotion, or an exciting romance could be yours for the taking.

June – Offers are streaming in. Take the time this month to sort them out and discard the least promising. You can't say 'yes' to everything.

July – Things are running smoothly. You're back in control, Rooster, and feeling good.

August – Time for a romantic holiday. Single Roosters go away with friends but find romance on foreign shores.

September – A glittering month. Roosters are in line for a promotion and extra cash.

October – Jealousy or divided loyalties could arise in the workplace. You may need to be diplomatic.

November – You're beginning to see the results of your efforts. You've got every reason to be proud.

December - Celebrations are in order, and your home becomes the centre of attention. You could be splurging on luxuries and treats. You've earned them. Enjoy.

Lucky Colours 2019: Scarlet, Gold, Chocolate Brown

Lucky Numbers 2019: 5, 7, 8

CHAPTER 12: THE DOG

Dog Years

14 February 1934 – 3 February 1935

2 February 1946 – 21 January 1947

18 February 1958 – 7 February 1959

6 February 1970 – 26 January 1971

25 January 1982 – 12 February 1983

10 February 1994 – 30 January 1995

29 January 2006 – 17 February 2007

16 February 2018 – 4 February 2019

Natural Element: Metal

Of all the animals in the Chinese zodiac, the dog is probably the easiest for us to understand. We welcome dogs into our homes, they accompany us on walks and trips, and in some cases they help with our work or, if we use a guide dog or a hearing dog, actually assist us with our daily lives.

Dogs are friends indeed.

Some people are afraid of dogs, of course, because they also come with sharp teeth and a loud bark but generally we're comfortable with canines in a way we wouldn't be with say a snake or a tiger.

To the Chinese, the sign of the Dog represents justice and compassion, and people born under the sign of the Dog are admired for their noble natures and fair-minded attitudes. Dogs will do the right thing even if it means they'll lose out personally. They have an inbuilt code of honour that they hate to break.

The Dog is probably the most honest sign of the zodiac. People instinctively trust the Dog even if they don't always agree with Dog's opinions. Yet Dogs are usually completely unaware of the high esteem in which they're held because they believe they're only acting naturally, doing the same that anyone else would do in the circumstances.

Since they have such a highly-developed sense of right and wrong, Dogs understand the importance of rules. Also, since deep down they're always part of a pack, even if it's invisible, Dogs know that fairness is vital. If there aren't fair shares all round, there's likely to be trouble they believe. So to keep the peace, Dog knows that a stout framework of rules is required and once set up, everyone should stick to them. Dogs are genuinely puzzled that other signs can't seem to grasp this simple truth.

People born under this sign tend to be physically strong with thick, glossy hair, and open, friendly faces. Their warm manner attracts new acquaintances but they tend to stay acquaintances for quite a while. It takes a long time for Dog to promote a person from acquaintance to real friend. This is because Dogs are one hundred percent loyal and will never let a friend down, so they don't give their trust lightly.

Dogs are intelligent and brave, and once they've made up their mind, they stick to it. They're quite prepared to go out on a limb for a good cause if necessary, but they don't really like being alone. They're much happier in a group, with close friends or family. What's more, though they're good managers, they're not interested in being in overall charge. They'd much rather help someone else achieve a goal than take all the responsibility themselves.

At work, Dog can be a puzzle to the boss. Though capable of immense effort and obviously the dedicated type, it's difficult to enthuse the Dog. Promises of pay rises and promotion have little effect. The Dog is just not materialistic or particularly ambitious in the conventional sense. Yet, if a crisis appears, if someone's in trouble or disaster threatens, the Dog is suddenly energised and springs into action. In fact, it's quite difficult to hold Dog back. Dogs will work tirelessly without rest or thought of reward until the rescue is achieved.

Bearing this in mind, Dogs would do well to consider a career that offers some kind of humanitarian service. This is their best chance of feeling truly fulfilled and happy at work.

At home, Dogs have a down to earth approach. Home and stability are very important to them. They're not the types to keep moving and trading up, but at the same time, they don't need their home to be a showcase. The Dog residence will be comfortable rather than stylish with the emphasis on practicality. Yet it will have a warm, inviting atmosphere, and the favoured visitors permitted to join the family there will be certain of a friendly welcome.

It's not easy to get Dog to take a break if there's a cause to be pursued, but when Dogs finally allow themselves to come off duty, they love to play. They like to be out in the open air or splashing through water and can discover their competitive streak when it comes to team games.

Best Jobs for Dog

Charity Worker

Nurse

Doctor

Teacher

Security Guard

Policeman

Fireman

Bank Clerk

Perfect Partners

Cupid's arrow can strike anywhere at any time, of course, but once the novelty of new romance wears off, some relationships are easier to maintain than others. Here's a guide to the Dog compatibility with other signs.

Dog with Dog

Dogs love company so these two will gravitate to each other and stay there. Both loyal, faithful types, neither need worry the other will stray. They'll appreciate their mutual respect for doing things properly and their shared love of a stable, caring home. This relationship is likely to last and last. The only slight hitch could occur if, over time, the romance dwindles and Dog and Dog become more like good friends than lovers.

Dog with Pig

In the outside world, the Dog and the Pig can get along well together; in fact, Pigs being intelligent creatures can do many of the things dogs can do, so it's not surprising this zodiac pair make a good couple. Good natured Pig is uncomplicated and fair-minded which suits Dog perfectly.

Also, Pig brings out Dog's playful side – which delights Pig who's always keen to have a playmate. A happy relationship involving many restaurants.

Dog with Rat

The Rat and the Dog get along pretty well together. Both strong characters, they respect each other and give each other space when required. But deep down, the Dog is a worrier and gets anxious about unnecessary risks, while Rat just can't help sailing close to the wind if an interesting opportunity presents itself. Long-term, reckless Rat might unintentionally drive Dog to distraction. Only to be considered by Dogs with nerves of steel.

Dog with Ox

These two ought to get along well as they're both sensible, down to earth, loyal, and hardworking, and in tune with each other's basic beliefs. And yet, somehow they don't. Dog has a playful streak and finds this lacking in Ox, while Ox may be baffled by what seems like pointless silliness in Dog. If they can agree to differ, they could make a relationship work.

Dog with Tiger

While not exactly opposites, these two are different enough to intrigue each other yet similar enough in basic outlook to get on well. Both Tiger and Dog are idealistic and uninterested in material gain yet where Dog can be nervous, Tiger's bold. And where Tiger attracts controversy, Dog will be loyal. This partnership could be lasting and valuable.

Dog with Rabbit

Despite the fact that in the outside world Rabbit could easily end up as Dog's dinner, the astrological pair gets on surprisingly well. Dog appreciates Rabbit's careful, efficient ways and soft voice, while Rabbit admires Dog's energy and good intentions. Dog's lack of interest in the finer points of interior design might try Rabbit's patience but with a little work, these two could reach an understanding.

Dog with Dragon

Not the easiest of combinations. Down-to-earth Dog can't see what all the fuss is about when it comes to Dragons. Unimpressed by glamour and irritated by what seems to Dog the gullibility of Dragon admirers,

Dog can't be bothered to find out more. Dragon meanwhile, is hurt by Dog's lack of interest. Great determination would be needed to make this work.

Dog with Snake

Some snakes seem to have an almost hypnotic power, and for some reason Dog is particularly susceptible to these skills. We've heard of snake-charmers but snakes can be dog-charmers and without even trying, Snakes can find themselves the recipients of Dog devotion. Since the Dog is strong, loyal, and can be fun, Snake is not averse to this but might, in the end, find it boring.

Dog with Horse

Both good friends of man, these two can make a formidable team. Dog understands the occasional need for solitude while admiring Horse's strength and agility. Horse, meanwhile, senses Dog's loyalty and down to earth nature. Both lovers of the great outdoors and physical activity, they'll never be short of adventures to share. A promising long-term relationship.

Dog with Goat

This is another relationship that could be tricky. Loyal Dog would be quite willing to stand by Goat when practical problems loom but could end up irritated by Goat's inability to learn from previous mistakes and so keeps making them. Goat can't understand why Dog gets so bothered. With care, these two could learn to live together.

Dog with Monkey

Monkey finds Dog intriguing. Monkey senses Dog's strength of character coupled with its playful streak which fits well with Monkey's love of games. Dog, meanwhile, appreciates Monkey's energy and light-hearted approach. Yet before long, Monkey's disdain for rules will grate on Dog's instinctive love of them. They cannot agree in this area, and it could lead to arguments.

Dog with Rooster

Rooster and Dog are not the best of partners. Dog can be as plain-spoken as Rooster and is not likely to be impressed by overt show. What's more, Dog is often critical and Rooster can't stand criticism. Rooster, on the other hand, is likely to sense and resent Dog's attitude.

Frustration abounds for both in this relationship. Only for the hopelessly love-struck.

Success For the Dog in The Year of the Pig

Well, Dog, your own special year is over, and the Pig rules 2019. So are you disappointed? Will you be sorry to hand over the steering wheel? Chances are most Dogs will be breathing a sigh of relief. They'll be glad to see the back of the Year of the Dog.

The reason is that (as counter-intuitive as it sounds) the Chinese believe a person's birth year is not necessarily the easiest of years for them. Perhaps like birth itself, the process of being born is immensely challenging though ultimately beneficial. Very few people wish it had never happened. So last year, many Dogs will have encountered big changes and situations which at times have been difficult. Yet, in years to come, when they look back, they will see that 2018 was the moment a whole new phase of their lives began.

At present, the shape of that new phase is probably not yet clear, but the Year of the Pig brings a welcome respite. The pressure's off. The Dog can sit back and put its paws up for a while, if it wishes, and just let the pieces fall into place around it.

The Pig and the Dog get on well. They're good friends. In fact, they share many similarities, and the Dog belongs to the Metal family of zodiac creatures which harmonises well with the Pig, regarded as a Water animal. What's more, the element of 2019 is Earth which encourages qualities such as loyalty, responsibility, and devotion to home – characteristics which are second-nature to the Dog – so Dogs will find the general tone of events easy to understand.

The Dog is probably the most conscientious and responsible of all the zodiac signs, yet typical Dogs may start the year feeling as if they've been carrying the world on their shoulders this past 12 months. In a sense, they have. So now they can drop that burden with a clear conscience.

Freedom is in the air for Dogs though it might take a few weeks for them to notice. When they look around, many Dogs will find either that their personal chalkboard has been wiped clean or that they are finally ready to start afresh in practically every area of their lives. A new career, a new home maybe, even a whole new set of friends is now a real possibility.

What's more, Dogs can expect a healthy financial boost. The enormous efforts made last year will pay off in 2019 big-time and the Dog will now have enough cash to get those dreams on the road.

Yet it's probably not a good idea to be too hasty, to begin with. In the year of the Pig, time is on Dog's side. After all the hard work of 2018, it's time for the Dog to relax and the Pig is the ultimate playmate.

The flip side to the Dog's conscientious nature is its love of games when work is over. Well, the work is over for a while now for typical Dogs, so they can indulge their frivolous, fun sides and be as silly as they like. Many Dogs will be inspired to take a series of delightful holidays – probably in the countryside, surrounded by hills and trees. Fresh air and open spaces will have a magnetic appeal as will picnics, parties, and games nights with friends. Eating out and elaborate eating in will also feature strongly. Quite a few Dogs are very good cooks and those that haven't yet tested their culinary skills could discover a new talent. Some Dogs could even be inspired to take part in a Bake Off-style competition or devise their own, with friends, for fun.

Most Dogs will still be going to work, of course, but there will be a noticeable easing of pressure. The Dog's previous efforts will be recognised and appreciated but, despite this, many Dogs will still be considering changing jobs or launching into a whole new career. More impatient types will take the chance to leap, but the others will have the luxury of plenty of time to consider their options, check out the opportunities, and maybe polish up their skills to enhance their chances for a big change next year.

The same goes for property. If they haven't already moved, many Dogs will find themselves wondering if they still want to live where they currently live even though they've previously been perfectly content there. Wise Dogs will enjoy themselves house-hunting and day-dreaming but not tying themselves down just yet.

All in all, the Dog can look forward to a very enjoyable year.

Love

Many single Dogs will find themselves single because a break-up occurred in the previous 12 months. Though this may have been traumatic, it has proved to be for the best. The strong, honest vibes of 2018 would not permit any treacherous behaviour to remain hidden, and many a relationship disintegrated when guilty secrets emerged. Yet, single Dogs can look forward to a carefree 12 months with new partners queuing up – attracted by the Dog's newfound playful air.

Single Dogs can enjoy 12 months of fun and frolicking.

Attached Dogs can congratulate themselves for managing to maintain their relationship through the ups and downs of the previous year. Having withstood all difficulties, yours is obviously a strong and worthwhile union. So, in 2019, the two of you can relax and rediscover all the things you enjoy doing together. Remind yourselves why you fell in love in the first place. Romantic weekends, and little breaks away, are all on the shopping list for 2019.

Keys to Success

Most Dogs will already be tasting success from the efforts they made last year and if, for some, it has not yet arrived, it is surely on its way. In 2019, success will come in the form of restoring balance and harmony to a lifestyle that's been too heavily weighted towards responsibilities. There's no point in being a rich, powerful Dog if you're too exhausted to appreciate your achievements. So, to make the most of 2019, Dogs should concentrate on leisure activities, healthy exercise, and good quality food. Work on your health and well-being Dog, and you'll have a wonderful year.

The Dog Year at a Glance

January – Things may seem a little slow, but you're beginning to sense something good is happening.

February – Work is getting interesting. An important person is taking an interest in you. There could be beneficial repercussions.

March – New friends are joining your circle – possibly colleagues who have become closer. Work and play begin to mix.

April – An authority figure can be a pain. They may not deserve respect, but remain tactful. Speaking bluntly could cause trouble.

May – A fascinating new face enlivens the love scene. Time to explore where this romance could lead.

June – Summer skies are calling. An excellent time to take a break with a special person.

July – Romance is going well. Watch out for a colleague or neighbour who loves to cause complications.

August – Another good time for a holiday or short break. Someone close may be breaking the rules. They may not listen to your good advice.

September – A rival at work could be trying to claim the credit that belongs to you. Skilful tactics are required.

October – Peace is restored, yet you may be feeling restless. House hunting or shopping for a new image is favoured.

November – Fun and games are on the menu. You're in the mood to party.

December – Festivities are hotting up, yet your to-do list is getting longer. Keep calm.

Lucky Colours for 2019: Flame, Gold, Brown
Lucky Numbers for 2019: 3, 4, 9

CHAPTER 13: THE PIG

Pig Years

4 February 1935 – 23 January 1936

22 January 1947 – 9 February 1948

8 February 1959 – 27 January 1960

27 January 1971 – 14 February 1972

13 February 1983 – 1 February 1984

31 January 1995 – 18 February 1996

18 February 2007 – 6 February 2008

5 February 2019 – 24 January 2020

Natural Element: Water

The last of the twelve signs of the zodiac, the Pig is probably the least popular of them all with people in the West. No one wants to tell their friends they're an astrological Pig. This useful, yet harmless, animal is so maligned; it attracts possibly more insults than any other creature.

Tell someone they 'eat like a pig' and you mean their table manners are atrocious, should they overindulge on food they're accused of being 'a greedy pig', if they stuff themselves with pizzas or burgers they're 'pigging out', and when their home's untidy they live in 'a pigsty'. Pigs are thought of as fat, unattractive, and dirty.

Yet left to themselves in the wild, pigs – while enjoying their food – are not particularly obese. They're intelligent and agile and can look after themselves very well.

In the East, the sign of the Pig is regarded as lucky and a little piglet arriving in the family is given a particularly warm welcome as it seems sure to grow into a happy person.

People born in the Year of the Pig are perhaps the most well-liked of all the signs. Cheerful, friendly, and lacking in ego, they have no enemies. They can fit in anywhere. Nobody objects to a Pig. Pigs just can't help being kind, sympathetic, and tolerant. Should someone let them down, Pigs will just shrug and insist it wasn't their fault. Pigs tend to get let down over and over again by the same people but it never occurs to them to bear a grudge. They forgive and forget and move happily along. Friends may scold and warn them not to be a soft touch but Pigs can't help it. They see no point in conflict.

That's not to say it's impossible to annoy a Pig, just that it takes a great deal to rouse the sweet Pig's nature to anger.

The other refreshing thing about the Pig is that they just want to be happy and have a good time – and they usually do. They find fun in the most unpromising situations and their enthusiasm is infectious. Soon everyone else is having fun too. It's true Pigs enjoy their food, perhaps a little too much, but that's because they are a sensuous sign, appreciating physical pleasures and it makes them very sexy too.

Shopping is a favourite hobby of many Pigs. They're not greedy, they just love spending money on pretty things simply for the sheer delight of discovering a new treasure and taking it home. This sometimes gets the Pig into trouble because finance isn't a strong point, but such is Pig's charm, they usually get away with it.

Pigs don't tend to be madly ambitious. They have no interest in the rat-race yet they are intelligent and conscientious and can't help being highly effective at work, despite having no ulterior motive or game plan. They often end up in a managerial role. Their sympathetic and conciliatory approach, coupled with their willingness to ask others for advice, goes down well in most organisations and usually leads to promotion. What's more, while avoiding unpleasantness wherever possible, the Pig doesn't like to give up on a task once started and will invariably find a way to get it done that other signs wouldn't have thought of.

The Pig home reflects the sensuous nature of the Pig. Everything will be comfortable and warm with fabrics and furnishings that feel good as well as look good. Items will be chosen for ease of use rather than style, and there will probably be a great many objects and knick-knacks dotted around, picked up on Pig's shopping expeditions. Pigs quite often excel at cooking and the Pig kitchen is likely to be crammed with all the latest gadgets and devices for food preparation.

Pigs approve of holidays, of course, and take as many as they can. They're not desperate to tackle extreme sports or go on dangerous expeditions but they can be adventurous too. They like to be out in the open air, especially if it involves picnics and barbecues but, basically, easy-going Pig's just happy to take a break.

Best Jobs for Pig

Cook

Restaurant Owner

Receptionist

Spa Therapist

Wedding Planner

Charity Worker

Manager

Perfect Partners

Cupid's arrow can strike anywhere at any time, of course, but once the novelty of new romance wears off, some relationships are easier to maintain than others. Here's a guide to the Pig's compatibility with other signs.

Pig with Pig

When one Pig sets eyes on another Pig, they can't help moving closer for a better look, and should they get talking they probably won't stop. These two understand each other and share so many interests and points of view they seem like a perfect couple. Yet, long-term, they can end up feeling too alike. Pigs rarely argue, yet oddly enough they can find themselves squabbling over trivialities with another Pig. Care needed.

Pig with Rat

It's very easy for Rat to be beguiled by the Pig. Pig's easy-going, sympathetic nature immediately relaxes the Rat. What's more, Pig loves shopping as much as Rat so the two of them could enjoy many happy expeditions together. Conflict could occur through overspending. Pig does not understand Rat's compulsion to bag a bargain. Pig will buy whatever the price and the two could end up arguing over money.

Pig with Ox

Delightful Pig will catch Ox's eye, and since Pig isn't a constant thrill-seeker, the two of them could enjoy many peaceful evenings together perhaps over a tasty meal. Yet Pig's spendthrift ways — at least in Ox's eyes — could soon prove very annoying as well as illogical to the Ox, while Pig could find Ox's attitude judgemental and upsetting. Not ideal for the long-term.

Pig with Tiger

Carefree Pig will love to bask in Tiger's impressive aura, while Tiger will feel good about protecting this charming but unworldly creature. They enjoy each other's company and Tiger, so focused on lofty matters, will find Pig's compulsive shopping too trivial to worry about. This couple could do well together as long as Pig's fondness for cosy nights in doesn't make Tiger feel trapped.

Pig with Rabbit

Pig is not quite as interested in fine dining as Rabbit, and is happy to scoff a burger as much as a cordon bleu creation, but their shared love of the good things in life makes these two happy companions. Once again, Pig's spending habits might irritate Rabbit, but not too much as Rabbit is quite willing to splurge on lovely things for the home. A relationship would work well.

Pig with Dragon

While Dragon and Pig might seem to be opposites, the two of them can create a surprisingly contented relationship. Pig is quite happy for Dragon to fly around doing exciting things as long as Pig is not expected to do much more than admire profusely. Dragon appreciates Pig's uncritical support and makes allowances for Pig's lack of stamina. This couple could live in harmony.

Pig with Snake

Pig and Snake don't have a lot to say to each other. Snake can't be bothered with Pig's endless shopping, and Pig is hurt by Snake's snobbish attitude. They both enjoy the good things in life so a luxury fling could briefly be fun — a shared spa break might be a good idea — but in the long-term, this relationship is probably not worth pursuing.

Pig with Horse

Pig and Horse are good companions. Horse is soothed by easy-going Pig and Pig is proud to be seen with such an alluring creature as Horse. They don't have a lot of interests in common but they don't antagonise each other either. They can jog along amicably for quite a while but long-term they may find they each want more than the other can provide.

Pig with Goat

Happy-go-lucky Pig and laid-back Goat make a good pair. They hate to stir up trouble and always look for a peaceful solution to any challenge. Ideally, they'd avoid the challenge altogether. They could be very contented together as long as Pig's spending and Goat's inability to deal with finances doesn't get them into trouble.

Pig with Monkey

On the surface, these two might seem an unlikely couple. Yet Pig enjoys Monkey's fun and humour while Monkey is happy to be admired uncritically. What's more, Monkey's inventive mind can solve any difficulties caused by Pig's spending and since Monkey can't resist a challenge, the opportunity to retrain Pig or at least find a way to obtain purchases cheaper could help the relationship last.

Pig with Rooster

These two might seem an unlikely couple – modest Pig with extrovert Rooster. Yet Pig has no need or wish to crow, and can see the vulnerable character that lurks beneath Rooster's fine feathers. While Rooster responds to Pig's kindness and undemanding nature. As long as Rooster doesn't get bored, this can be a contented relationship.

Pig with Dog

In the outside world, the dog and the pig can get along well together; in fact, pigs, being intelligent creatures, can do many of the things dogs can do, so it's not surprising this zodiac pair make a good couple. Good natured Pig is uncomplicated and fair-minded which suits Dog perfectly. Also, Pig brings out Dog's playful side – which delights Pig who's always keen to have a playmate. A happy relationship involving many restaurants.

Success For the Pig in The Year of the Pig

Congratulations, Pig! It's your year. The whole of 2019 is shot through with those wonderful qualities that come naturally to you, because they represent your true character. Your fabulous sign brings good luck and good cheer to the rest of the zodiac and, for the next 12 months, your values rule.

This is how the world felt the year you were born, so 2019 ought to have a comfortable, familiar atmosphere. Make the most because you won't get a chance to be top sign for another 12 whole years.

This is all good news, of course, yet oddly enough, when your birth sign year comes around, the Chinese don't regard it as the best ever year for that particular sign. It's not necessarily the easiest year you'll ever enjoy.

Perhaps, it is similar to how many of us view our birthdays. As well as being a day of celebration, it is often also a day when we look back over the year and reflect on our achievements, goals, mistakes, and the direction in which we hope to move in the coming 12 months; accordingly, the return of our birth-year sign signals the beginning of a similar review.

Pigs will find themselves looking back over the past decade and a bit, back to 2007, the last Year of the Pig and consider what's happened since then. There will have been a great many changes, many events both good and bad; from this perspective, the Pig will be able to see whether the choices they made at the time worked well, or whether certain things could have been handled better. Has life been progressing as the Pig hoped or are there adjustments that could now be made to improve things?

While the other signs are in party mood, the Pig is likely to be more reflective than usual. Nevertheless, even a slightly subdued Pig is still full of fun, and there will be plenty of enjoyment for Pigs in 2019. It's just that this year, Pigs are looking to the future more than they've probably done for a very long time.

Chances are, the typical Pig will notice that finances are not a Pig strong point. Pig spending is lavish whether or not there are funds in the bank and this has probably led to problems now and again, over the years. In 2019, many Pigs could find themselves restructuring their financial affairs and making a sustained effort to cut down on impulse buying. Like other signs, the Pig could well receive a cash boost this year, but more sensible individuals will decide to take expert advice before splurging the lot.

Career Pigs will have done well in 2018. Their friendly, easy-going personalities make them popular with co-workers; even boss-Pigs are liked and, together with their loyalty, these characteristics will have led to advancement. During 2019, most Pigs will be consolidating their positions, while at the same time wondering if they intend to spend the next 12 years in the same role. Pigs like to feel settled, so these thoughts could be uncomfortable, but they realise they may need to make a change sometime soon.

The same goes for the place they live. Pigs are not particularly worldly and aren't out to impress, but some Pigs could notice their home is not as comfortable as it used to be. Perhaps the area has changed or is not as convenient as it was; perhaps Pig has outgrown the space, or perhaps the building itself is in need of repair. Since comfort is of prime importance to the Pig, this can become a serious issue. Much as they hate the upheaval, many Pigs could find themselves actually contemplating making a move this year.

Pigs thrive with a familiar routine which is why all this emphasis on re-arranging their lives – even in order to make improvements – is likely to prove stressful at times. Yet there are plenty of compensations. Some of the extra cash can be spent on soothing breaks, and many a Pig will find themselves winding down on a luxury cruise or two in 2019. Nothing relaxes a Water animal like being out on a calm, warm sea.

The other antidote to stress for a Pig, of course, is food and Pigs are likely to enjoy even more delicious meals than usual in 2019.

Love

The Pig is a very sensuous sign and single Pigs could find themselves much in demand this year. The Year of the Pig has lent all Pigs even more star quality than usual, and the other signs really can't get enough of Pig company. What's more, with Pig stress raised slightly higher than normal in 2019, single Pigs are keen to soothe their nerves with long, candle-lit dinners, lots of cuddles, and long hours in the bedroom. The Pig soulmate could well appear this year and may be discovered at some sort of family gathering.

Strangely for such a peaceful sign, attached Pigs could find themselves having a few arguments with their partners in 2019. These are likely to be caused simply by the additional stress the Pig feels when considering potential changes. It may be, also, that Pig's partner has become so accustomed to Pig's settled ways, they don't understand why things suddenly need to be different. With give and take on both sides, the discord will soon be settled, and Pig and partner will kiss and make up.

Keys to Success

For the Pig, in the Year of the Pig, the secret of success can probably be summed up in one word – restraint. Restraint in all things. Since all the Pig's qualities (both good and bad) are emphasised this year, Pig's own negative qualities will be magnified on a personal level too. That means over-spending and over-eating will prove extremely difficult to resist – yet resist you must if you want to do well in 2019.

Pigs could also experience more stress than usual this year and being sensitive creatures need to make sure they build some regular, calming activities into their schedule.

The Pig Year at a Glance

January – You're surrounded by friends as your year begins, and you can look forward to 12 months of popularity.

February – Children and babies figure prominently in the last days of winter, bringing much joy.

March – Finances need care. A loan or arrangement involving money seems to hit a hold up.

April – a partner proves unexpectedly stubborn. Consider their point of view. Tact and diplomacy work wonders.

May – Watch out for a tempting romance that may not live up to its promise. Is this person being truthful?

June – Improvements can be made and the way is becoming clear.

July – Expert advice can sort out issues involving finance, investments, and property. Don't be afraid to ask.

August – You're forming a plan, but it's making you nervous. A relaxing holiday will be the tonic you need.

September – Now is the month to make your move or embark on some training or educational course.

October – Should you find a new home or stay put? You're confused. Listen to well-meaning advice, but don't necessarily take it.

November – Finances need attention again. Make a sensible budget and stick to it.

December – It looks like there's more in the bank than you realised. An ideal state of affairs for the festive season.

Lucky Colours 2019: Red, White, Yellow

Lucky Numbers 2019: 2, 5, 8

CHAPTER 14: BUT THEN THERE'S SO MUCH MORE TO YOU

So now you know your animal sign, but possibly you're thinking – okay, but how can everyone born in the same year as me have the same personality as me?

You've only got to think back to your class at school, full of children the same age as you, to know this can't be true. And you're absolutely right. What's more, Chinese astrologers agree with you. For this reason, in Chinese astrology, your birth year is only the beginning. The month you were born and the hour of your birth are also ruled by the twelve zodiac animals – and not necessarily the same animal that rules your birth year.

These other animals then go on to modify the qualities of your basic year personality. So someone born in an extrovert Tiger year but at the time of day ruled by the quieter Ox, and in the month of the softly spoken Snake, for instance, would very likely find their risk-taking Tiger qualities much toned down and enhanced by a few other calmer, more subtle traits.

By combining these three important influences, you get a much more accurate and detailed picture of the complex and unique person you really are. These calculations lead to so many permutations it soon becomes clear how people born in the same year can share various similarities, yet still remain quite different from each other.

What's more, the other animals linked to your date of birth can also have a bearing on how successful you will be in any year and how well you get on with people from other signs. Traditionally, the Horse and the Rabbit don't get on well together, for instance, so you'd expect two people born in these years to be unlikely to end up good friends. Yet if both individuals had other compatible signs in their charts, they could find themselves surprisingly warming to each other.

This is how it works:

Your Outer Animal – (Birth Year | Creates Your First Impression)

You're probably completely unaware of it, but when people meet you for the first time, they will sense the qualities represented by the animal that ruled your birth year. Your Outer Animal and its personality influence the way you appear to the outside world. Your Outer animal is your public face. You may not feel the least bit like this creature deep down, and you may wonder why nobody seems to understand the real you. Why is it that people always seem to underestimate you, or perhaps overestimate you, you may ask yourself frequently. The reason is that you just can't help giving the impression of your birth-year animal and people will tend to see you and think of you in this way – especially if they themselves were born in other years.

Your Inner Animal – (Birth Month | The Private You)

Your Inner Animal is the animal that rules the month in which you were born. The personality of this creature tells you a lot about how you feel inside, what motivates you, and how you tend to live your life. When you're out in the world and want to present yourself in the best light, it's easy for you to project the finest talents of your birth-year animal. You've got them at your fingertips. But at home, with no one you need to impress, your Inner Animal comes to the fore. You can kick back and relax. You may find you have abilities and interests that no one at work would ever guess. Only your closest friends and loved ones are likely to get to know your Inner Animal.

By now you know your Outer Animal so you can move on to find your Inner Animal from the chart below:

Month of Birth - Your Inner Animal

January – the Ox

February – the Tiger

March – the Rabbit

April – the Dragon

May – the Snake

June – the Horse

July – the Goat

August – the Monkey

September – the Rooster

October – the Dog

November – the Pig

December – the Rat

Your Secret Animal – (Birth Hour I The Still, Small Voice Within)

Your secret animal rules the time you were born. Each 24-hour period is divided into 12, two-hour time-slots and each slot is believed to be ruled by a particular animal. This animal represents the deepest, most secret part of you. It's possibly the most intimate, individual part of you as it marks the moment you first entered the world and became 'you'. This animal is possibly your conscience and your inspiration. It might represent qualities you'd like to have or sometimes fail to live up to. Chances are, no one else will ever meet your Secret Animal.

For your Secret Animal check out the time of your birth:

Hours of Birth – Your Secret Animal

1 am – 3 am – the Ox

3 am – 5 am – the Tiger

5 am – 7 am – the Rabbit

7 am – 9 am – the Dragon

9 am – 11 am – the Snake

11 am – 1.00 pm – the Horse

1.00 pm – 3.00 pm – the Goat

3.00 pm – 5.00 pm – the Monkey

5.00 pm – 7.00 pm – the Rooster

7.00 pm – 9.00 pm – the Dog

9.00 pm – 11.00 pm – the Pig

11.00 pm – 1.00 am – the Rat

When you've found your other animals, go back to the previous chapters and read the sections on those particular signs. You may well discover talents and traits that you recognise immediately as belonging to you in addition to those mentioned in your birth year. It could also be that your Inner Animal or your Secret Animal is the same as your Year animal. A Dragon born at 8 am in the morning, for instance, will be a secret Dragon inside as well as outside, because the hours between 7 am and 9 am are ruled by the Dragon.

When this happens, it suggests that the positive and the less positive attributes of the Dragon will be held in harmony, so this particular Dragon ends up being very well balanced.

You might also like to look at your new animal's compatibility with other signs and see where you might be able to widen your circle of friends and improve your love life.

CHAPTER 15: IN YOUR ELEMENT

There's no doubt about it, Chinese astrology has many layers, but then we all recognise that we have many facets to our personalities. We are all more complicated than we might first appear. And more unique too.

It turns out that even people who share the same Birth Year sign are not identical to people with the same sign but born in different years. A Rabbit born in 1963, for instance, will express their Rabbit personality in a slightly different way to a Rabbit born in 1975. This is not simply down to the influence of the other animals in their chart, it's because each year is also believed to be ruled by one of the five Chinese 'elements' as well as the year animal.

These elements are known as Water, Wood, Fire, Earth, and Metal.

Each element is thought to contain special qualities which are bestowed onto people born in the year it ruled, in addition to the qualities of their animal sign.

Since there are 12 signs endlessly rotating and five elements, the same animal and element pairing only recurs once every 60 years. Which is why babies born in this 2018 year of the Brown Dog are unlikely to grow up remembering much about other Earth Dogs from the previous generation. The senior Dogs will already be 60 years old when the new pups are born.

In years gone by, when life expectancy was much lower, the chances are there would only ever be one generation of a particular combined sign and element alive in the world at a time.

Find Your Element from the Chart Below

The 1920s

5 February 1924 – 24 January 1925 | RAT | WOOD

25 January 1925 – 12 February 1926 | OX | WOOD

13 February 1926 – 1 February 1927 | TIGER | FIRE

2 February 1927 – 22 January 1928 | RABBIT | FIRE

23 January 1928 – 9 February 1929 | DRAGON | EARTH

10 February 1929 – 29 January 1930 | SNAKE | EARTH

The 1930s

30 January 1930 – 16 February 1931 | HORSE | METAL

17 February 1931 – 5 February 1932 | GOAT | METAL

6 February 1932 – 25 January 1933 | MONKEY | WATER

26 January 1933 – 13 February 1934 | ROOSTER | WATER

14 February 1934 – 3 February 1935 | DOG | WOOD

4 February 1935 – 23 January 1936 | PIG | WOOD

24 January 1936 – 10 February 1937 | RAT | FIRE

11 February 1937 – 30 January 1938 | OX | FIRE

31 January 1938 – 18 February 1939 | TIGER | EARTH

19 February 1939 – 7 February 1940 | RABBIT | EARTH

The 1940s

8 February 1940 – 26 January 1941 | DRAGON | METAL

27 January 1941 – 14 February 1942 | SNAKE | METAL

15 February 1942 – 4 February 1943 | HORSE | WATER

5 February 1943 – 24 January 1944 | GOAT | WATER

25 January 1944 – 12 February 1945 | MONKEY | WOOD

13 February 1945 – 1 February 1946 | ROOSTER | WOOD

2 February 1946 – 21 January 1947 | DOG | FIRE

22 January 1947 – 9 February 1948 | PIG | FIRE

10 February 1948 – 28 January 1949 | RAT | EARTH

29 January 1949 – 16 February 1950 | OX | EARTH

The 1950s

17 February 1950 – 5 February 1951 | TIGER | METAL

6 February 1951 – 26 January 1952 | RABBIT | METAL

27 January 1952 – 13 February 1953 | DRAGON | WATER

14 February 1953 – 2 February 1954 | SNAKE | WATER

3 February 1954 – 23 January 1955 | HORSE | WOOD

24 January 1955 – 11 February 1956 | GOAT | WOOD

12 February 1956 – 30 January 1957 | MONKEY | FIRE

31 January 1957 – 17 February 1958 | ROOSTER | FIRE

18 February 1958 – 7 February 1959 | DOG | EARTH

8 February 1959 – 27 January 1960 | PIG | EARTH

The 1960s

28 January 1960 – 14 February 1961 | RAT | METAL

15 February 1961 – 4 February 1962 | OX | METAL

5 February 1962 – 24 January 1963 | TIGER | WATER

25 January 1963 – 12 February 1964 | RABBIT | WATER

13 February 1964 – 1 February 1965 | DRAGON | WOOD

2 February 1965 – 20 January 1966 | SNAKE | WOOD

21 January 1966 – 8 February 1967 | HORSE | FIRE

9 February 1967 – 29 January 1968 | GOAT | FIRE

30 January 1968 – 16 February 1969 | MONKEY | EARTH

17 February 1969 – 5 February 1970 | ROOSTER | EARTH

The 1970s

6 February 1970 – 26 January 1971 | DOG | METAL

27 January 1971 – 14 February 1972 | PIG | METAL

15 February 1972 – 2 February 1973 | RAT | WATER

3 February 1973 – 22 January 1974 | OX | WATER

23 January 1974 – 10 February 1975 | TIGER | WOOD

11 February 1975 – 30 January 1976 | RABBIT | WOOD

31 January 1976 – 17 February 1977 | DRAGON | FIRE

18 February 1977 – 6 February 1978 | SNAKE | FIRE

7 February 1978 – 27 January 1979 | HORSE | EARTH

28 January 1979 – 15 February 1980 | GOAT | EARTH

The 1980s

16 February 1980 – 4 February 1981 | MONKEY | METAL

5 February 1981 – 24 January 1982 | ROOSTER | METAL

25 January 1982 – 12 February 1983 | DOG | WATER

13 February 1983 – 1 February 1984 | PIG | WATER

2 February 1984 – 19 February 1985 | RAT | WOOD

20 February 1985 – 8 February 1986 | OX | WOOD

9 February 1986 – 28 January 1987 | TIGER | FIRE

29 January 1987 – 16 February 1988 | RABBIT | FIRE

17 February 1988 – 5 February 1989 | DRAGON | EARTH

6 February 1989 – 26 January 1990 | SNAKE | EARTH

The 1990s

27 January 1990 – 14 February 1991 | HORSE | METAL

15 February 1991 – 3 February 1992 | GOAT | METAL

4 February 1992 – 22 January 1993 | MONKEY | WATER

23 January 1993 – 9 February 1994 | ROOSTER | WATER

10 February 1994 – 30 January 1995 | DOG | WOOD

31 January 1995 – 18 February 1996 | PIG | WOOD

19 February 1996 – 7 February 1997 | RAT | FIRE

8 February 1997 – 27 January 1998 | OX | FIRE

28 January 1998 – 5 February 1999 | TIGER | EARTH

6 February 1999 – 4 February 2000 | RABBIT | EARTH

The 2000s

5 February 2000 – 23 January 2001 | DRAGON | METAL

24 January 2001 – 11 February 2002 | SNAKE | METAL

12 February 2002 – 31 January 2003 | HORSE | WATER

1 February 2003 – 21 January 2004 | GOAT | WATER

22 January 2004 – 8 February 2005 | MONKEY | WOOD

9 February 2005 – 28 January 2006 | ROOSTER | WOOD

29 January 2006 – 17 February 2007 | DOG | FIRE

18 February 2007 – 6 February 2008 | PIG | FIRE

7 February 2008 – 25 January 2009 | RAT | EARTH

26 January 2009 – 13 February 2010 | OX | EARTH

The 2010s

14 February 2010 – 2 February 2011 | TIGER | METAL

3 February 2011 – 22 January 2012 | RABBIT | METAL

23 January 2012 – 9 February 2013 | DRAGON | WATER

10 February 2013 – 30 January 2014 | SNAKE | WATER

31 January 2014 – 18 February 2015 | HORSE | WOOD

19 February 2015 – 7 February 2016 | GOAT | WOOD

8 February 2016 – 27 January 2017 | MONKEY | FIRE

28 January 2017 – 15 February 2018 | ROOSTER | FIRE

16 February 2018 – 4 February 2019 | DOG | EARTH

5 February 2019 – 24 January 2020 | PIG | EARTH

The 2020s

25 January 2020 – 11 February 2021 | RAT | METAL

12 February 2021 – 1 February 2022 | OX | METAL

2 February 2022 – 21 January 2023 | TIGER | WATER

22 January 2023 – 9 February 2024 | RABBIT | WATER

10 February 2024 – 28 January 2025 | DRAGON | WOOD

29 January 2025 – 16 February 2026 | SNAKE | WOOD

17 February 2026 – 5 February 2027 | HORSE | FIRE

6 February 2027 – 25 January 2028 | GOAT | FIRE

26 January 2028 – 12 February 2029 | MONKEY | EARTH

13 February 2029 – 2 February 2030 | ROOSTER | EARTH

You may have noticed that the 'natural' basic element of your sign is not necessarily the same as the element of the year you were born. Don't worry about this. The element of your birth year takes precedence, though you could also read the qualities assigned to the natural element as well, as these will be relevant to your personality but to a lesser degree.

Metal

Metal is the element associated in China with gold and wealth. So if you are a Metal child, you will be very good at accumulating money. The Metal individual is ambitious, even if their animal sign is not particularly career-minded. The Metal-born version of an unworldly sign will still somehow have an eye for a bargain or a good investment; they'll manage to buy at the right time when prices are low and be moved to sell just as the price is peaking. If they want to get rid of unwanted items, they'll potter along to a car boot sale and without appearing to try, somehow make a killing, selling the lot while stalls around them struggle for attention. Career-minded signs with the element Metal have to be careful they don't overdo things. They have a tendency to become workaholics. Wealth will certainly flow, but it could be at the expense of family harmony and social life.

The element of Metal adds power, drive, and tenacity to whatever sign it influences so if you were born in a Metal year you'll never lack cash for long.

Water

Water is the element associated with communication, creativity, and the emotions. Water has a knack of flowing around obstacles, finding routes that are not obvious to the naked eye and seeping into the smallest cracks. So if you're a Water child, you'll be very good at getting what you want in an oblique, unchallenging way. You are one of nature's lateral thinkers. You are also wonderful with people. You're sympathetic, empathetic, and can always find the right words at the right time. You can also be highly persuasive, but in such a subtle way nobody notices your influence or input. They think the whole thing was their own idea.

People born in Water years are very creative and extremely intuitive. They don't know where their inspiration comes from, but somehow ideas just pour into their brains. Many artists were born in Water years.

Animal signs that are normally regarded as a little impatient and tactless have their rough edges smoothed when they appear in a Water year. People born in these years will be more diplomatic, artistic, and amiable than other versions of their fellow signs. And if you were born in a naturally sensitive, emotional sign, in a Water year, you'll be so intuitive you're probably psychic. Yet just as water can fall as gentle nurturing rain, or a raging destructive flood, so Water types need to take care not to let their emotions run away with them or to allow themselves to use their persuasive skills to be too manipulative.

Wood

Wood is the element associated with growth and expansion. In Chinese astrology, Wood doesn't primarily refer to the inert variety used to make floorboards and furniture, it represents living, flourishing trees and smaller plants, all pushing out of the earth and growing towards the sky.

Wood is represented by the colour green, not brown. If you're a Wood child, you're likely to be honest, generous, and friendly. You think BIG and like to be involved in numerous projects, often at the same time.

Wood people are practical yet imaginative and able to enlist the support of others simply by the sincerity and enthusiasm with which they tackle their plans. Yet even though they're always busy with a project, they somehow radiate calm, stability, and confidence. There's a sense of the timeless serenity of a big old tree about Wood people. Other signs instinctively trust them and look to them for guidance.

Animal signs that could be prone to nervousness or impulsive behaviour tend to be calmer and more productive in Wood year versions, while signs whose natural element is also Wood could well end up leaders of vast teams or business empires. Wood people tend to sail smoothly through life, but they must guard against becoming either stubborn or unyielding as they grow older or alternatively, saying 'yes' to every new plan and overextending themselves.

Fire

Fire is the element associated with dynamism, strength, and persistence. Fire demands action, movement, and expansion. It also creates a huge amount of heat. Fire is precious when it warms our homes and cooks our food, and it possesses a savage beauty that's endlessly fascinating. Yet it's also highly dangerous and destructive if it gets out of control. Something of this ambivalent quality is evident in Fire children.

People born in Fire years tend to be immensely attractive, magnetic types. Other signs are drawn to them. Yet there is always a hint of danger, of unpredictability, about them. You never know quite where you are with a Fire year sign and in a way, this is part of their fascination.

People born in Fire years like to get things done. They are extroverted and bold and impatient for action. They are brilliant at getting things started and energising people and projects. Quieter signs born in a Fire year are more dynamic, outspoken, and energetic than their fellow sign cousins, while extrovert signs positively blaze with exuberance and confidence when Fire is added to the mix.

People born in Fire years will always be noticed, but they should try to remember they tend to be impatient and impulsive. Develop a habit of pausing to take a deep breath to consider things, before rushing in, and you won't get burned.

Earth

Earth is the element associated with patience, stability, and practicality. This may not sound exciting but, in Chinese astrology, Earth is at the centre of everything: the heart of the planet. Earth year children are strong, hardworking personalities. They will persist with a task if it's worthwhile and never give up until it's complete. They create structure and balance, and they have very nurturing instincts.

Women born in Earth years make wonderful mothers, and if they're not mothering actual children, they'll be mothering their colleagues at work, or their friends and relatives, while also filling their homes with houseplants and raising vegetables in the garden if at all possible.

Other signs like being around Earth types as they exude a sense of security. Earth people don't like change, and they strive to keep their lives settled and harmonious. They are deeply kind and caring and immensely honest. Tact is not one of their strong points, however. They will always say what they think, so if you don't want the unvarnished truth, better not to ask!

Earth lends patience and stability to the more flighty, over-emotional signs, and rock solid integrity to the others. Earth people will be sought-after in whatever field they choose to enter, but they must take care not to become too stubborn. Make a point of seeking out and listening to a wide range of varying opinions before setting a decision in stone.

Yin and Yang

As you looked down the table of years and elements, you may have noticed that the elements came in pairs. Each element was repeated the following year. If the Monkey was Water one year, it would be followed immediately the next year by the Rooster, also Water.

This is because of Yin and Yang – the mysterious but vital forces that, in Chinese philosophy, are believed to control the planet and probably the whole universe. They can be thought of as positive and negative, light and dark, masculine and feminine, night and day, etc. but the important point is that everything is either Yin or Yang; the two forces complement each other and both are equally important because only together do they make up the whole. For peace and harmony to be achieved, both forces need to be in balance.

Each of the animal signs is believed to be either Yin or Yang and because of the need for balance and harmony, they alternate through the years. Six of the 12 signs are Yin and six are Yang and since Yang represents extrovert, dominant energy, the Yang sign is first, followed by the Yin sign which represents quiet, passive force. A Yang sign is always followed by a Yin sign throughout the cycle.

The Yang signs are:

Rat

Tiger

Dragon

Horse

Monkey

Dog

The Yin Signs are

Ox

Rabbit

Snake

Goat

Rooster

Pig

Although Yang is seen as a masculine energy, and Yin a feminine energy, in reality, whether you are male or female, everyone has a mixture of Yin and Yang within them. If you need to know, quickly, whether your sign is Yin or Yang just check your birth year. If it ends in an even number (or 0) your sign is Yang. If it ends in an odd number, your sign is Yin.

In general, Yang signs tend to be extrovert, action-oriented types while Yin signs are gentler, more thoughtful, and patient.

So, as balance is essential when an element controls a period of time, it needs to express itself in its stronger Yang form in a Yang year as well as in its gentler Yin form in a Yin year, to be complete.

That's why this year of the Earth Dog (Yang) will be followed next year in 2019 by the Earth Pig (Yin) before the Earth element is complete and the stage is set for Metal in 2020.

But why do elements have two forms? It's to take into account the great variations in strength encompassed by an element. The difference between a candle flame and a raging inferno – both belonging to Fire; or a great oak tree and a little seedling – both belonging to the Wood element.

In Yang years, the influence of the ruling element will be particularly strong.

Friendly Elements

Just as some signs get on well together and others don't, so some elements work well together while others don't. These are the elements that exist in harmony:

METAL likes EARTH and WATER

WATER likes METAL and WOOD

WOOD likes WATER and FIRE

FIRE likes WOOD and EARTH

EARTH likes FIRE and METAL

The reason for these friendly partnerships is believed to be the natural, productive cycle. Water nourishes Wood and makes plants grow, Wood provides fuel for Fire, Fire produces ash which is a type of Earth, Earth can be melted or mined to produce Metal while Metal contains or carries Water in a bucket.

Unfriendly Elements

But since everything has to be in balance, all the friendly elements are opposed by the same number of unfriendly elements. These are the elements that are not in harmony:

METAL dislikes WOOD and FIRE

WATER dislikes FIRE and EARTH

WOOD dislikes EARTH and METAL

FIRE dislikes METAL and WATER

EARTH dislikes WOOD and WATER

The reason some elements don't get on is down to the destructive cycle which is: Water puts out Fire and is absorbed by Earth, Wood breaks up Earth (with its strong roots) and is harmed by Metal tools, Metal is melted by fire and can cut down Wood.

So if someone just seems to rub you up the wrong way, for no logical reason, it could be that your elements clash.

CHAPTER 16: CREATE A WONDERFUL YEAR

By now, you should have got a pretty good idea of the main influences on your life and personality according to Chinese astrology. But how is 2019 going to shape up for you? Well, that largely depends on how cleverly you play your hand. The Year of the Pig is traditionally a fortunate year for all the signs and certainly less intense than 2018, but some signs will find the conditions ahead more favourable than others. This is always the case, but it's what you do with the conditions that counts.

Sit back and rely on good fortune alone, if it's an easier year for your sign, and you could snatch failure from the jaws of success. Navigate any stormy seas with skill and foresight if, it's not such a sunny year for your sign, and you will sail on to fulfil your dreams.

The future is not set in stone.

Chinese astrology is used very much like a weather forecast, so that you can check out the likely conditions you'll encounter on your journey and plan your route and equipment accordingly. Some might need a parasol and sandals; while others, stout walking boots and rain-gear. Yet properly prepared, both will end up in a good place at the end of the trip.

Finally, it's said that if you feel another sign has a much better outlook than you this year, you can carry a small symbol of that animal with you (in the form of a piece of jewellery, perhaps, or a tiny charm in your pocket or bag) and their good luck will rub off on you. Does it work? For some, maybe, but there's no harm in trying.

Other Books from Bennion Kearny

Finding Your Way Back to YOU: A self-help book for women who want to regain their Mojo and realise their dreams!

Are you at a crossroads in life, lacking in motivation, looking for a new direction or just plain 'stuck'?

Finding your Way back to YOU is a focused and concise resource written specifically for women who have found themselves in any of the positions above.

The good news is that you already have all of the resources you need to solve your own problems; this practical book helps you remove the barriers that prevent this from happening.

The Savvy Traveller Survival Guide

The Savvy Traveller Survival Guide offers practical advice on avoiding the scams and hoaxes that can ruin any trip.

From no-menu, rigged betting, and scenic taxi tour scams to rental damage, baksheesh, and credit card deceits – this book details scam hotspots, how the scams play out and what you can do to prevent them. *The Savvy Traveller Survival Guide* will help you develop an awareness and vigilance for high-risk people, activities, and environments.

Forewarned is forearmed!

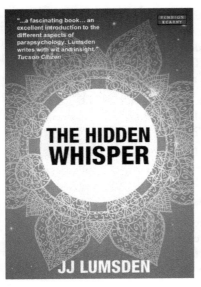

The Hidden Whisper

Want to dive into the paranormal and learn about Extra Sensory Perception, Psychokinesis, Ghosts, Poltergeists and more, but don't know where to start?

The Hidden Whisper is the acclaimed paranormal thriller, written by real-life parapsychologist Dr. JJ Lumsden, which offers a rare opportunity to enter the intriguing world of parapsychology through the eyes of Luke Jackson. The poltergeist narrative is combined with extensive endnotes and references that cover Extra Sensory Perception, Psychokinesis, Haunts, Out of Body Experiences, and more.

From Dinner Date to Soulmate – Cynthia Spillman's Guide to Mature Dating

Are you reaching a more mature stage in life and looking for a new relationship? Are you tentatively returning to the dating arena following the end of a relationship? Do you want to successfully find the man of your dreams and avoid the many pitfalls?

This book is for you.

Written by international dating coach Cynthia Spillman, founder of The International Dating Academy and formerly the Chief Executive of Dinner Dates, *From Dinner Date to Soulmate* is a humorous, practical, and inspirational handbook for the growing mature dating market.

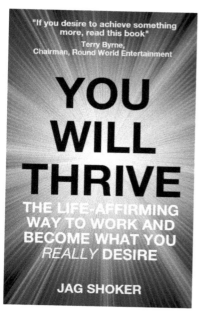

You Will Thrive: The Life-Affirming Way to Work and Become What You Really Desire

You Will Thrive addresses the subject of modern disillusionment. It is essential reading for people looking to make the most of their talents and be something more in life. Something that matters. Something that makes a difference in the world.

Through six empowering steps, it reveals 'the Way' to boldly follow your heart as it leads you to the perfect opportunities you seek. Through every step, it urges you to put a compelling thought to the test:

You possess the power within you to attract the right people, opportunities, and circumstances that you need to become what you desire.

Write From The Start: The Beginner's Guide to Writing Professional Non-Fiction

Do you want to become a writer? Would you like to earn money from writing? Do you know where to begin?

Help is at hand with *Write From The Start* – a practical must-read resource for newcomers to the world of non-fiction writing. It is a vast genre that encompasses books, newspaper and magazine articles, press releases, business copy, the web, blogging, and much more besides.

Jam-packed with great advice, the book is aimed at novice writers, hobbyist writers, or those considering a full-time writing career, and offers a comprehensive guide to help you plan, prepare, and professionally submit your non-fiction work. It is designed to get you up-and-running fast.

CPSIA information can be obtained
at www.ICGtesting.com
Printed in the USA
BVHW070804020119
536776BV00020B/3932/P